OFF
THE
RECRD

OFF THE RECORD

SECRETS TO BUILDING A
SUCCESSFUL
RETIREMENT AND A
LASTING LEGACY

ADAM CUFR, RICP®

Published by Advantage, Charleston, South Carolina.
Member of Advantage Media Group.

ADVANTAGE is a registered trademark and the Advantage colophon is a trademark of Advantage Media Group, Inc.

Printed in the United States of America.

ISBN: 978-159932-408-1
LCCN: 2013955465

This publication is designed to provide accurate and authoritative information in regard to the subject matter covered. It is sold with the understanding that the publisher is not engaged in rendering legal, accounting, or other professional services. If legal advice or other expert assistance is required, the services of a competent professional person should be sought.

Advantage Media Group is proud to be a part of the Tree Neutral® program. Tree Neutral offsets the number of trees consumed in the production and printing of this book by taking proactive steps such as planting trees in direct proportion to the number of trees used to print books. To learn more about Tree Neutral, please visit www.treeneutral.com. To learn more about Advantage's commitment to being a responsible steward of the environment, please visit www.advantagefamily.com/green

Advantage Media Group is a publisher of business, self-improvement, and professional development books and online learning. We help entrepreneurs, business leaders, and professionals share their Stories, Passion, and Knowledge to help others Learn & Grow. Do you have a manuscript or book idea that you would like us to consider for publishing? Please visit advantagefamily.com or call 1.866.775.1696.

I dedicate this book to my best friend, loving wife, and extraordinary mother to our daughters. We've endured so much together and your strength continues to amaze me.

And to my parents, who somehow magically seem to know when to speak and when to listen. You're some of the best in the parenting business.

TABLE OF CONTENTS

About the Author

Adam Cufr, RICP®, is a founding principal of Fourth Dimension Financial Group, LLC, an author, a sought-after media commentator, and thought leader. Adam was named one of twenty Most Creative People in Insurance in 2015 and is a columnist for *Retirement Advisor Magazine*.

Adam has been featured in national publications such as the *Wall Street Journal, Senior Market Advisor Magazine, LifeHealthPro*, as well as locally in the *Toledo Blade,* the *Defiance Crescent News,* and the *Bryan Times*. Adam writes the "Beyond the Money" column in the *Suburban Press* and has been frequently interviewed on the WTOL Channel 11's "More for Your Money" segment, often offering not-so-common common sense on a variety of financial topics.

After beginning his career at the world headquarters of a Fortune 500 company based in St. Louis, Adam spent the next ten years in various financial services businesses, deepening his knowledge with each experience. Fourth Dimension Financial Group is the culmination of the best of those experiences and seeks to replace much of the complexity that exists in retirement planning with clarity of thinking. As a result, Adam is invited regularly to speak about and teach financial concepts at events and workshops.

Adam has earned licenses in life, health, and property and casualty insurance, as well as the Series 6, 7, 24, 26, and 63 licenses. He also earned the American College's prestigious Retirement Income Certified Professional® (RICP®) designation. Adam graduated from

Bowling Green State University with business management degrees in purchasing materials management and production operations management. He is a native of Northwood, Ohio, and in 2012 was chosen as Alumnus of the Year by Northwood High School.

Married since 1999, Adam and his wife, Carie are on a grand adventure with six daughters. Adam enjoys working out, reading thought-provoking books, and driving sports cars. For twenty years, Adam performed as a drummer in the Ohio Air National Guard Band of the Great Lakes. Drumming has allowed Adam to perform in six countries, on national television, with Miss America, and for the president of the United States.

Your Financial Opus

You are holding this book in your hands right now because you have an interest in making wise decisions concerning your financial future and possibly your retirement. This is an exciting pursuit and one that should be taken with great care. While I'm not a financial expert, I have had some unique experiences that led me to reconsider the very nature of what retirement can mean to people.

I have witnessed our church grow from a core group of 25 people into a regular attendance of around 10,000 in just over 18 years. It has been an amazing opportunity to see people grow to experience more of the purpose and fulfillment God intended for their lives. What's their secret for finding purpose? Service to others.

As I have watched thousands of volunteers serving passionately—many in the second half of their lives—while thousands more sit on the sidelines, I have often asked myself:

"Would people feel more comfortable serving others if they knew they had their own planning in order?"

I believe they would. See, for most of human history, people were born, they worked, and they died. Retirement, as we know it, is a relatively new concept. What I seek to do is create opportunities for people to passionately serve others, leading to more fulfilling lives for the server and the served. In this book, Adam seeks to offer the financial tools necessary to help people achieve enough, financially. Once they cross that point, a different point for everyone, will they feel more comfortable serving others with passion and purpose?

Every day I see the effects of changed lives. Every day, I pray for changed hearts. If you have already retired or if retirement is in your near future, I encourage you to arm yourself with the tools necessary to achieve your own enough so that you may be freed up to offer your unique gifts to the world. That's how lives are changed. That's how hearts are transformed.

As you read this book, don't be surprised if you feel called to find your own place of service and are forever changed in the process.

Lee Powell
Founding Pastor
CedarCreek.tv
One Church Multiple Campuses

A Different Drummer

"If a man does not keep pace with his companions, perhaps it is because he hears a different drummer. Let him step to the music which he hears, however measured or far away."

—Henry David Thoreau

Something about the drums in the corner of the cafeteria called to me, and I knew I had to check them out. I think of that boyhood scene often, as if it were a photograph etched into my memory by a flashbulb.

My classmates and I had been brought to the school cafeteria to consider whether we wanted to play an instrument. Various choices were set up in an array around the cafeteria, and the drum practice pad was hardly the most attractive of the lot. But it drew me like a magnet, and thus I began my drumming career.

I had plenty of doubts about whether I was cut out to be a drummer. After some time in the band program, I distinctly remember looking down the line of drummers. There were so many of them, and they all seemed better than me. I wondered why I was there. I couldn't hope to be as good as they were.

Years later, it occurred to me that they were all gone. They had all quit. They had all moved on to something else or decided drumming wasn't for them, and I remained, drumstick in hand. I became a high-level player in all the honors groups.

I felt driven to improve, to reach an ever higher level, transformed by a drum set. That's what I have been doing ever since. As the years went by, I kept the beat while my classmates set their sticks aside.

I did not exactly start with a bang, though. At first I hated the thought of even 20 minutes of practice a day. The mechanics frustrated me. Still, I persisted. Then, one Christmas, I opened a package to find a pair of drumsticks in a cardboard cylinder, and tied to them was a key.

"Go downstairs," my parents said, "and you'll see where that key fits." In the basement, I saw a lock on a door that previously had not had one. I unlocked the door, and inside the room was the drum set of my dreams. My parents added a stipulation to the gift: to keep that drum set, I would need to take private lessons. They had recognized my keen interest, and they had the wisdom to know I needed someone to push me and drive me to be my best.

Soon there came a day when I found that I could do a pretty decent job with a Led Zeppelin song. Pretty cool, I thought, pretty cool. And it was then that I was transformed from a guy who hated practicing 20 minutes a day into one who was willing to practice for three hours a day. I had a fire in me, and I have it to this day.

I find a rare and special joy in the music. When I am playing what's in me, I feel an energy welling up and surging through my entire body. It is transcendent and truly joyful, beyond what I could have imagined as I struggled at that practice pad. Drumming has been a beautiful dimension in my life, and my parents long ago helped me unlock that passion and taught me that I needed others to take me where I couldn't take myself. They fanned the flame that became the fire.

OTHER DIMENSIONS

I have been blessed with a musical persistence and vision that has enriched my life. In my career, I also see every day how persistence and vision and clarity of goals can enhance the lives of my clients. I am a financial advisor who specializes in assisting those who are embarking on retirement, and I see common themes in both my avocation and my occupation.

Both music and financial planning are highly creative processes with clear structures but with other elements that are as ineffable as inspiration. It is inspiration that above all I hope to impart to my readers, although to each individual what matters most will be different. We all, however, need others to help us on our journey. We need to work with our fellow bandsmen so that we all can perform our best.

In my firm, Fourth Dimension Financial Group, located in Perrysburg, Ohio, I help retirees with a critical part of financial planning that calls for a specialist. I place a heavy emphasis on making sure that the money they have accumulated during their working years will produce a reliable income for the rest of their lives.

"I have been blessed with a musical persistence and vision that has enriched my life. In my career, I also see every day how persistence and vision and clarity of goals can enhance the lives of my clients."

Income planning is one of four distinct aspects—the four dimensions—to successful retirement preparation. The other dimensions are risk and fee analysis, a forward-looking tax review, and estate and legacy planning. As people make plans to convert their portfolios into a retirement income, they need to understand how taxes can significantly influence how much they will have to spend. They need to know how much risk they can accept without compromising their security and how fees can deplete their income potential. And they need to determine what will become of their estate once they pass on, whether it is transitioned to family or charity or both.

In this book, we'll take a closer look at all of those dimensions as well as the dimension of time, which often is considered the fourth dimension beyond the three spatial ones. So much of our financial life is contingent on time.

I have been in the retirement planning business for about 13 years as I write this, and I think even my grade-school classmates had me sized up for the kind of career I would have. When I was in fifth grade, one of my classmates told me, "You are Alex P. Keaton," the Family Ties character played by Michael J. Fox. He was the guy with monogrammed pajamas and a briefcase. So I guess I was always seen by others as having kind of a business or financial acumen. And that played out: I have a business degree and I worked for three years at a Fortune 500 company in St. Louis as a purchasing manager. We built large-scale chemical facilities not only in the South but also in Brazil.

My wife, Carie, and I were a young, married couple then, and we saved a large percentage of our income, in part because I did not really care for my job and I wanted to get out of the game. One day, two men with whom I played racquetball—a financial rep for Northwestern Mutual and an advisor with Edward Jones—signed me up as a client. Seeing my natural interest, they encouraged me to try financial services as a career, and I was intrigued. My wife was able to leave her PhD program early, but with a master's degree, and I quit my corporate job. We moved to Ohio to be close to family. We were ready to start our own family and I launched my new career.

It might seem that I was unwise to up and leave a corporate job with all the perks—and have my spouse quit a PhD program—so that I could be a commission-only financial services rep, but I felt driven. At first I worked as a "captive agent," meaning I was a representative for only one firm's products, and I sensed that I was on the wrong path there. I wanted to be able to offer whatever products and services were best for the client, whether my company sold them or not. So I became an independent advisor.

PLAYING TO THE AUDIENCE

All the while, I kept drumming. I played the full complement in concert band settings. I did that for 20 years in the Air National Guard band in the US Air Force. I have played big band and a variety of other styles, but my passion is rock drumming as a drum set player. I have gone from playing in bars to performing before big audiences.

I'd had my moment of soul searching when, after high school, I auditioned for music school and also applied for business school and was offered both. It was perhaps the first really adult decision I had to make. I chose to pursue business as my primary vocation and music as a hobby but a very serious hobby with a longtime commitment to the US Air Force.

I think that being really good at one thing can translate to other pursuits. It takes discipline to learn any craft—the fundamentals, the whats and the whys. You need to be able to focus long enough to gain experience and competence. Many people never get there. They feign competence. They fake it but never make it.

To live and work responsibly, one must go deeper. Your band is relying on you. It needs to know you will maintain the tempo and the groove. I have learned that in music, and I have learned that in financial services. My clients need to know that I am sensitive to their timing and that I have good structure as well as the creativity to rise above just the basics. It is essential to know the rules. It is an art to be able to creatively apply those rules to someone's personal situation for the best possible outcome.

I have been open, in life, to going where the music takes me. I have performed for the president of the United States and for the president of Hungary. I kept the beat at Mount Rushmore on the

Fourth of July, and with Miss America in a rock concert. I have a CD on iTunes. I have been fortunate to gain wide experience, both military and nonmilitary, as I have played to audiences time and time again.

FROM THE OLD WORLD TO THE NEW

In fact, one of my ancestors was also a military drummer. My mother has done extensive genealogy research. My six-times great-grandfather on her side, Meshach, served as a military drummer during the Revolutionary War until his capture at the Battle of Germantown. After 11 months in prison, he returned to his regiment and was one of four men chosen as a "life guard to the commander in chief." He served in Gen. George Washington's personal entourage until the end of the war. Upon learning that, I felt intimately connected with the past. It felt as if not just a blood line had been passed down to me but a passion.

I am a blond in a family with dark hair. I do not look much like my parents or brothers. I used to joke with my mom that maybe I was adopted. "I remember the day you were conceived," she told me, "and I assure you, you are not adopted." And yet I felt different as a child, and I have always been more intense than most people. It can be hard for me to just let loose, so I find joy in structured activities that let me go deep and rise high. That connection with my past held special meaning for me.

It led me to thinking about what the immigrants from the Old World faced as they adjusted to life in the New World. I've seen some old pictures that my mother found, and we have connected with family members who still live in the Czech Republic. We began to correspond, and at family gatherings we read letters from them even though the translation can sometimes be less than perfect.

What struck me was the nature of the transition. In both music and financial planning, much of what I do is about transition. In drumming I am captivated by the transitions from one section of a song to the next. That's the drum fill. We've got a groove, and the groove's happening. We need the fill to transition us from the chorus to the verse or to the bridge.

"What struck me was the nature of the transition. In both music and financial planning, much of what I do is about transition."

And as I help people with their finances, transition is also a key element. For 30 or 40 years, they worked for a paycheck, and now they will need to convert their savings to income when those paychecks stop. How will they make that transition?

Through my experience, I have become well versed in dealing with transitions. It is how I am wired. It is how I think, how I view life. My own life has been transition after transition. And as I looked at those old photographs that my mother showed me, I thought about the transitions of our ancestors. I looked at the faces of my grandmother and grandfather on my dad's side. At Ellis Island, we found their records, and their names had been changed as they came through. It struck me that immigrants left everything behind to have a new life, either fleeing the bad or pursuing the great. It was a balance of pitfalls and possibilities.

When we are doing retirement planning, almost all of our clients come to us from some other advisor, and those other advisors typically specialized in helping them to accumulate money. Now these clients are in their 50s, 60s or 70s and accumulation no longer is the goal. As retirement specialists, we focus on distributing money.

In other words, we are here for the transition. Change can be difficult, and I recognize that my clients often are leaving advisors they have worked with for a long time. We are grateful for the work that they have done, but this is the new world. It requires new languages, new customs, new strategies, new dress, new words. Much has to change for you to be able to adapt and survive in this world, in which you no longer work for a living.

I think that's one of the reasons we are so good at what we do: We help people who are ready for change, who need assistance to survive in the new world. We're not the right solution for everyone, and we know that, but for the right clients at the right time we excel.

A BIRTH OF EMPATHY

On April 17, 2004, life gave my wife and me a profound experience that forever shaped me as a man, as a father, as a husband and as a professional. I'd thought of myself as a pretty good guy, but I was intense and driven, that middle child who overachieves. I needed more compassion and empathy for people who did not share that level of intensity. My wife, Carie, is just as much of an achiever as me, if not more so.

We'd started a family, and everything went perfectly with the birth of our first daughter, Anna. It was going well too when Carie was pregnant with our second daughter, Catherine, and we felt fully prepared. The nursery was set up, and we were ready.

But one Saturday morning, when the baby was nearly full-term, Carie did not seem quite herself. I asked her what was going on.

"I haven't felt Catherine move in about a day and a half," she told me. "I'm very scared."

"What does this mean?"

"I think we should go and get it checked out," Carie said. She told me she had been up all night, praying.

I canceled a business meeting scheduled that morning, and we drove in silence to the hospital, where a nurse began an ultrasound. We'd had a lot of ultrasounds, but this time the nurse seemed particularly intense as she searched and searched on the screen.

"I'm going to get the doctor," she finally said. "I'll be right back." Carie and I looked at each other. I followed the nurse into the hallway, and I saw that she was running to the nurses' station. Soon, a doctor came in and checked for a heart rate on the monitor and did not say anything.

"Did you find the heartbeat?" I said after a while.

"No."

I lost it. I broke down, and when I composed myself, I looked at Carie as she lay there.

"This must be God's will," she said. "What now?"

I thought, as I looked at her, "Who is this person?"

The doctor told us that they would be inducing labor and that Carie would give birth that day to a dead child. Catherine Rose was 7 pounds, 11 ounces. We got to hold our daughter for nearly an hour before handing her to a nurse, never to see her precious face again.

In the many painful months that followed, it seemed that I found that extra measure of compassion. I developed a deeper empathy. I realized that each one of us has a story. As we rush around, planning our finances, playing our music, smiling or crying, we all have a story behind our faces. And my own story doesn't end there. You might think that would have been our share of suffering. You would think we could have said, "God, thank you for showing us about compassion. We know that our daughter, without sin, is at your side."

Carie became pregnant two more times. Nora and Rosalie both were born perfectly healthy. And then Carie found she was pregnant again, this time with twins. At sixteen weeks, the doctor told us that our twins were suffering from something called twin-to-twin transfusion syndrome and there was about a 20 percent chance that they would survive. Carie needed a lot of bed rest, and every week for nine weeks we had to drive for two and a half hours to a hospital in Columbus, Ohio, for procedures administered by a specialist. Carie gave birth three months prematurely to our fourth and fifth daughters—one was 1 pound 11 ounces, and the other was 1 pound 5 ounces—and they began fighting for their lives. They were micro-preemies; they were the length of your hand, and looked like baby birds, with see-through skin. This began Carie's daily trips to the hospital to be reunited with her daughters. Evelyn struggled and remained in the hospital for almost a year.

That was in February 2009. The twins are nine years old now, and doing fine, but it was another of those experiences that bring you face to face with who you really are, and who really is in control of your life. When you realize how utterly powerless you are, that's when you feel a surge of incredible confidence and perseverance. You find a quiet strength. I felt deeply grateful, and from those struggles I also gained empathy for people who are going through tough times.

TO THE HEART OF THINGS

Life changes. We experience transitions and transformations, and we need to be mindful of that.

Our planning needs to reflect that. As we look to the future, we need to build in flexibility. Yes, we want to prepare for certain outcomes, but we need a Plan B, and a Plan C. As a musician, I know that when you are performing, the unexpected happens. Having that stage presence and the experience to know how to handle things will give the people around you confidence. They will know that they can trust you to make it through to the bow. They will know that you have seen it all before and that you gave it everything you had because you care deeply.

Retirees, and those nearing retirement, can face a multitude of worries. Retirement in itself is a time of great transition. It can be frightening. The recent economic turmoil has been daunting. "Will I have enough to make it through?" "Will I have to go back to work?" Be encouraged. When you think everything is lost, you can find a way. There's much to learn, and much you can do.

My own experiences led me to change my focus and build a practice specializing in retirement planning. Retirees often feel vulnerable, and I understand that feeling. I understand the level of planning and the level of trust needed to provide the reassurance for a happy retirement. I feel a kinship, and I share with my clients what I have been through. When I let them in on who I really am, they let me in on who they really are and when I know that, I can plan all the better on their behalf.

"My own experiences led me to change my focus and build a practice specializing in retirement planning. Retirees often feel vulnerable, and I understand that feeling. I understand the level of planning and the level of trust needed."

It can be hard to help those who come looking for a cookie-cutter approach as in, "Just show me the boxes to check and the lines to fill out." That limits them. Far better to pour out your concerns. Clients came to me in 2009, in the wake of economic troubles, and cried, "What do we do?" I felt great satisfaction in knowing that I could comfort them. "We'll work through this," I told them. "There are always options. There's always a tomorrow. There's always another opportunity." It is a role that calls for the human touch.

It is not easy to be vulnerable and people can feel that way when I ask them to open their hearts and tell me what they truly want out of retirement. What would bring the most meaning to the rest of their lives? I think sometimes that people believe such openness could make them susceptible to criticism. I let them know that I am here to serve them, and to do so I will rally all my experience and competence and heart. And that's what they are looking for. They want an advisor who knows the right strategies and products but who also will draw out of them what their goals are for retirement and who will walk them through the process of reaching those goals.

I have seen them share their hopes and their fears and I have seen their tears, many times. These are matters that grip the heart as people come to terms with what really matters in life and what it all has meant. Sometimes they are looking, for the first time, at their legacy. I might be sitting with a widow, for example, or someone who has cancer, and she is trying to put her affairs in order and the pain is very near the surface. I keep a box of tissues nearby. I do not inspire people to cry, but I am willing to go there with them. Not everyone wants to get deep, and we do not force the issue. But when things get real—when we get to the heart of things—we can begin to accomplish a lot.

MISSION POSSIBLE

This is our mission statement: Fourth Dimension Financial Group exists to help people seeking financial retirement achieve enough, live fully, and help others do the same. That statement is pregnant with meaning to me. "Helping people seeking financial retirement" is a deliberate choice of words because retirement means something different to everyone.

Retirement to some means, "I am done. I am going to lie back and enjoy life, and I do not ever intend to work for money again." That's certainly a distinct choice. For others, financial retirement is simply knowing they do not have to work for money, but they may choose to continue to do so or work in a capacity in which they do not need to request money. Financial retirement is the point at which you can stop working for money if you choose.

The time when you "achieve enough" is subjective and different for everyone. That's based on your experiences, and on your concerns, and on what you would like financial retirement to look like. "Enough" is unique to you. It is one of the big questions that people have. "Do we have enough?" I often hear. The answer is, "It depends"—and that's where the planning process really begins to take shape.

We also strive to help people live fully, and to me that means living free of worries about money to the extent that you can disconnect emotionally from finances and invest that emotional capital into the things that you are passionate about. Perhaps that is serving others, or a dedication to a cherished cause. We want to draw out what is important to people so that they can devote themselves to it, free of the worry of ever running out of money.

Retirement also is a time to help others. If you feel you have found some of the answers in life, why keep them to yourself? I encourage people to invite others to visit with us, to come to our client gatherings and educational events. If you have discovered insights for a worry-free financial retirement, share them with your family, friends, and coworkers. We can serve our clients better when we all participate in the experience.

Our clients typically are between the ages of 55 and 75, either nearing retirement or already into it. Generally, they own a business or hold a key position in somebody else's business. In general they are conservative by nature, though they may take an aggressive stance in some aspects of life. They are interested in making things simpler and more transparent, when possible, and they want to dig in to find truth and wisdom in their endeavors.

As far as concerns the level of a client's assets that we work with, we have had little need to define a minimum because people nearing retirement tend to have a fair amount of assets. On the low end, we work with people who have $100,000, but most of the people we work with generally have between $500,000 and $3 million of assets that they would invest.

We have clients from many walks of life. Interestingly, we have a strong clientele of engineers, which I find gratifying because they are the type of people who want the most data and the most rational, factual information. We seem to attract them because of our commitment to our process. Many professionals are accustomed to process. Pilots have their flight plans; scientists have the scientific method; engineers have what they call DMAIC (which stands for "define, measure, analyze, improve, control). They find that we too have a process that befits their way of thinking.

THE GOOD STEWARD

We help to structure a retirement plan that can protect a lifetime of accumulated assets so that retirees can live free of financial worry, short of a collapse of the entire economy. They can stress-test their plan by subjecting it to various scenarios: How would it do if this happened? Or if that happened? "Would I still have enough money?" Our planning is robust and flexible enough to address those concerns and hold up to such tests.

A lot of people out there, who claim to do retirement planning, are not addressing it that way. They are looking at how various funds and stocks and financial products have been performing, but they do not recognize the need for a planning structure that can minimize risk. Our process brings it all together in a way not addressed by a lot of financial planners.

Think of it like this: If you knew that you were missing a critical fact that could either cost you a significant amount of money or create a great opportunity for you, when would you want to know about that? I think you would want to know about that right away, if not yesterday. As you read this book, my hope is to bring you information that can change your course for the better. You may wish you had known about these matters long ago, but even now they can help to lead you to a brighter future. It is advice that not only can save you a lot of money but ultimately may free you from a lot of heartache.

"Think of it like this: If you knew that you were missing a critical fact that could either cost you a significant amount of money or create a great opportunity for you, when would you want to know about that?"

In this book, you will learn some things that may surprise you. Here are just a few:

- Although the S&P gained over 8 percent in the last 20 years, the actual performance was 4.25 percent over that period for those who invested all in equities, and 2.29

percent for stock and bond investors. They do not get the full market performance. Why?

- For years, many advisors have trumpeted that you can safely withdraw 4 or 4.5 percent from your portfolio annually in retirement without much risk. That's based on the historical return for the United States. Other nations have had significantly lower rates. Do you believe the United States will remain an economic superpower, or do you see a developing world economy that soon could level the playing field?

- Even if you believe that withdrawing 4 percent is a safe bet, what if you retire in a year—such as 2007, for example— and see your portfolio immediately plummet for a year or two? If you are spending money from that account but no longer are contributing to it, what happens to your retirement security? How will such a tough blow, early on, change the course of your retirement?

- Are mutual funds really a good place to invest for retirement, as many people believe? How much are high fees sapping your nest egg? Are there ways to invest that will allow you to keep more while taking the same risk, or to keep the same while significantly lowering your risk?

- Many retirees lose out because of a widespread belief that they should keep most of their assets liquid during retirement so that they are available for spending if need be. That's a strategy based on fear. Fearful people stuffed money in mattresses during the Great Depression and for years afterward, only to eventually see that inflation, that insidious menace, had eaten much of it away.

When you are approaching retirement, you need a foundation of financial certainty as you look toward new pursuits. You may have interests and hobbies and relationships and acts of service that you have long wanted to develop, and this will be your opportunity. Like a musician in a band or orchestra, you will bring your talents to the fore as you play harmoniously with others.

The various elements of your retirement plan likewise need to work in concert. It will be composed of distinct components—different types of products, and assets—with each designed to fulfill a particular need or desire, whether it is paying the monthly bills, saving for a trip, or leaving money for the kids or charity. It is important that your money meet your goals and that those financial products be used where they will serve you best, not where they never were designed to be used. If each of those instruments is played properly, you will attain a unified whole. You can feel confident that you have taken care of yourself.

When you build your plan correctly, you not only can take care of yourself and meet your aspirations, but you may find that you have the resources to take care of others. You could well have something significant to leave behind. Perhaps that will be financial assets. And perhaps it will be a bounty of wisdom for the next generation to build upon. In that way, you become a successful steward, gaining the maximum benefit for yourself and for those who follow.

Your retirement plan is indeed your financial opus, a major composition of balance and beauty that will determine the course of your elder years and that could determine how you will be remembered for generations to come.

"When you build your plan correctly, you not only can take care of yourself and meet your aspirations, but you may find that you have the resources to take care of others. You could well have something significant to leave behind."

CHAPTER 1

Tempo: Setting the Proper Pace for Retirement

"Half our life is spent trying to find something to do with
the time we have rushed through life trying to save."

—Will Rogers

So many retirees anticipate this new chapter of life with such
grand hopes. They will be done with work! They will have
time, time, time—finally!—to do all the things they have
dreamed of doing. And a month later, many tell me: "I'm bored out
of my mind." They find themselves doing odds and ends around the

house, and eventually they go out to find a part-time job. They are casting about for some purpose in retirement.

There are other retirees, however, who have a game plan. They feel even busier than when they were working. Perhaps they are donating their time in acts of service, whether doing volunteer work for organizations, mentoring young people, or helping with the grandkids. They develop new interests and pursue them. They are clear about their life goals and feel dedicated to attaining them. They are active and busy, but it is a different kind of busy than when they headed off to work each day.

Different people have different ideas of the retirement lifestyle, of course, and I make no judgment there. Some relish the thought that they are "done," now, after forty years of service, and it is time to enjoy the fruits of that labor. They want to relax and have some fun for a change. Others want to fill every hour. The trick is to understand your true needs and desires and whether the lifestyle you would pursue will really work for you. And you must be confident that your financial resources are adequate for your endeavors.

The bored retiree is not the happy retiree. After years of identifying oneself by one's career, retirement can lead not only to boredom but to loss of identity. You may feel you have lost your sense of belonging and value. All those talents, all those skills you honed through years on the job—what becomes of them now? If those feelings go unmanaged, they can be harmful to your health. Studies have shown they can reduce your longevity. By contrast, when retirees remain very active, they tend not to feel that they have lost their identity and purpose. They soon take on a new identity and often it is one that they have long wanted. They are fulfilling those pent-up ambitions.

Clearly, then, a successful retirement is not all about finances and investments. Yes, you need the money to match your lifestyle. But you need the lifestyle that will fulfill you, and you should be thinking about that long before you get that final paycheck. Time on your hands is a valuable asset. A meaningful identity is a valuable asset. The ability to serve others is a valuable asset.

"Clearly, then, a successful retirement is not all about finances and investments. Yes, you need the money to match your lifestyle. But you need the lifestyle that will fulfill you."

All musicians know the importance of tempo. What makes a musical work unique and special has much to do with the space between the notes: the silence, the variation. Without variation, you have flat-line noise. When you add variation, whether through volume or periods of rest or tempo changes, you give life to the music. That's the way it is with people too. In planning your retirement, you must be cognizant of the tempo. You need to get the timing right.

As you can see, I am a man of two passions: music and finances. I perceive parallels and metaphors in many aspects of both. I have been a drummer for a long time. Some people assume that keeping the tempo is the drummer's only job. It is certainly a fundamental. But for seasoned drummers, getting the tempo correct is a given, and then they get the chance to add color, shape, and other nuances to the music. I think of that when I help clients create their financial plan for retirement. I help them find the beat by which they can plan their days ahead. When a drummer sets the proper pace, he helps to bring out the best in the other musicians so that they can better express more of themselves. They need that foundation. So do retirees.

THE RETIREMENT BOOM

The baby boomers are beginning to retire in droves. In fact, approximately 10,000 people in the United States reach retirement age every day, a figure that certainly will continue to blossom as those born in the postwar years of 1946 to 1964 reach their mid-60s. A lot more people are retiring than ever before, and they are living a lot longer. As the baby boom wave ripples forward, it creates a broad financial marketplace that caters to retirees and their needs.

The Social Security Administration's own statistics indicate that in 2036, the system as it stands today would be able to pay only 77 percent of promised benefits. For a person who today is 43 years old, that year could be a milestone where benefits will have to be reduced, barring any gradual adjustments beforehand. The system is suffering from the tide of new retirees claiming benefits while fewer workers remain to support them. The handwriting is on the wall for the Social Security system, and retirees will need to depend more and more on their own investments to see them through.

The nature of those investments is bound to change, as well, as the economy shifts. As the exodus from the workforce continues, fewer people will be contributing to the economy. With so many people reaching a point in their lives when they want and need and deserve to slow down a bit, we will experience—in the words an economist would use—a falloff in productivity. The markets could increasingly reflect that, and investors will want to consider those implications.

NEW RULES, NEW WORRIES

For those who are entering retirement, it is a new territory. This is a new phase of life, with different rules. The way that they long were accustomed to investing and handling money may not serve them well now as the focus shifts from accumulating money to distributing it.

"For those who are entering retirement, it is a new territory. This is a new phase of life, with different rules."

Retirement is an exciting time, as you are on the brink of having the freedom to do some of things that you long have dreamed about. But for many it is also a troubling time.

It is very healthy to talk things through with other people who may have experienced the same feelings. How did they cope with that loss of their work identity? How did they settle on their retirement goals? Some people dislike the thought of goals, but certainly we all would like to derive some meaning from those days when our agenda isn't set for us and we can decide for ourselves how to fill the hours. What will be the milestones by which you measure your journey?

All those possibilities may come laden with doubts. When I sit down with people who are contemplating retirement, I see genuine excitement on their faces, but in their eyes I often see fear, as well. "This is it," they often are thinking. "This is my final stretch in life. What if I screw this up? What if retirement isn't all it is cracked up to be? What if living my dream turns out to be a nightmare? What if the economy crashes? What if taxes or inflation bleed me dry?"

"When I sit down with people who are contemplating retirement, I see genuine excitement on their faces, but in their eyes I often see fear, as well."

Those indeed are sobering questions, and it is important to consider such matters well before the final paycheck. When you still have money hitting the bank account, a do-over is relatively easy. But in retirement it could be prohibitively expensive, and changing course dramatically could have serious consequences. You need to address those matters head on.

In essence, what is different financially about retirement is that you are moving from that period of your life when your focus was on building for the future. The future has arrived. You will now be using the money you worked to save. That is a significant shift, and your portfolio must reflect that new directive. The tools, the products, the strategies must change dramatically. The way you invested to sock away your money should not be the same way that you invest as you begin spending it. In fact, if you do not adjust those strategies, you could be jeopardizing your life savings and the lifestyle in retirement that you dreamed of.

For decades you deferred gratification as you focused on immediate concerns and set money aside. Now those dreams no longer need be deferred. However, the mindset of saving and building doesn't easily evolve into a mindset of preserving and enjoying what you have built. For some people, that is very difficult. You need to address not only the nuts and bolts of retirement planning but also the emotional and lifestyle issues involved, and you need a special relationship with an advisor to help you address both aspects.

FROM YOUTH TO MATURITY

I think of a person's financial life as having three distinct phases: the saving, investing, and maturity phases. When you were young, you learned about banks. Perhaps someone took you to open an account and deposit your allowance and save up for something special. That's how you learned to defer the gratification of a candy bar for the eventual reward of a bike. You learned to live on less than you had.

As time went by, you got a job and had an income and a little extra money. Soon, perhaps, you were introduced to the worlds of Wall Street and mutual funds and life insurance and other ways to make money grow. You had your first experience with investments, and for the next 30 or 40 years your focus was on growing your money—and dealing with the many expenses involved in growing your life. Perhaps you married, had kids, bought a house and took on debt, and more debt, until you wondered how you would ever pay it off. You were concerned about keeping a reliable job and advancing in your career to maintain that lifestyle.

Then you woke up to find that the kids had grown. They were more or less financially independent of Mom and Dad. You realized that you didn't have all that many years remaining until you reached retirement age, and you began to assess whether you had accumulated enough. You began to think about slowing down, and your outlook changed from how to make and save enough to using what you accumulated. That is when you entered the maturity phase.

How do you know that you are moving into the maturity phase? Let's say today the stock market goes down 30 percent and so does your portfolio. Well, if you are 26 years old, what do you do? Chances are you go home, talk about it with your spouse over dinner, and you go back to work the next day and you get another paycheck. But how does that 30 percent decline in the market feel when you are 62 or 68? You might flip out. You fret. You get on the phone hoping to find a way to fix this.

When you feel that way about it, you know that you are nearing or are in the maturity phase. That's a good barometer. Each phase has its own distinct opportunities and challenges, as we have discussed. If you have picked up this book to read, chances are that you are nearing that maturity phase—and congratulations.

When things always go well, planning isn't necessary. They do not always go well and that's why planning is critical. That is what we are doing here. We are beginning to understand what could go wrong in that maturity phase and how you can protect yourself and prosper. You want your dreams to come true. You want to be able to be fully you.

"When things always go well, planning
isn't necessary. They do not always go well
and that's why planning is critical."

THE TICKING CLOCK

When you were young, your biggest asset was time. You had time on your side then. You could afford more aggressive investments, you could afford more risk. As you get older, you do not have that much time. I don't mean that as a morbid reminder that your days are numbered; it is simply a mathematical fact in our finite lives. When your time is relatively short you have to think differently about your investments.

I recently listened to an episode of Jerry Seinfeld's web series *Comedians in Cars Getting Coffee*, in which his guest was Alec Baldwin. In his mid-50s, Baldwin said he'd always had a list of things to do in life but now he *really* wanted to do them because he had less time left.

That struck me. We put things off. Along with aging comes wisdom, and we feel more demands upon us. As we succeed, more people want access to us. As our families grow, we feel more obligations. We increasingly worry about allocating our time, whereas in youth, time seemed endless. Time gains in value and meaning when you have less of it. When your remaining days are fewer, you want the quality of your time to be higher.

You must think about that compression of time in your investment life, as well. If you no longer will be contributing regularly to an investment account and if, in fact, you are withdrawing from it, any fluctuations of the market that affect that account will have a profoundly different effect on your savings. That is the principle of reverse dollar cost averaging, which I will discuss later in this book.

A PARADE OF WORRIES

When retirees are polled (see appendix) about their worries and fears, the most common fear is running out of money. They are more concerned about that than they are about dying. They fear that they will live too long and outlast the money they need to see them through their final years.

"When retirees are polled (see appendix) about their worries and fears, the most common fear is running out of money."

It is natural to worry about running out of money, even if you have plenty. Many people who recently reached retirement age were slammed by the stock market in 2007 and 2008. They had trusted in the market for decades, and on the eve of retirement it let them down, not to mention their portfolios. The market can seem like an uncontrollable beast waiting to pounce. People imagine years of savings erased because a rogue trader pushes the wrong button or terrorists strike again or the government comes out with a surprise policy. They are understandably more concerned about such risks, real or perceived, when those savings represent all they have for the rest of their lives.

Retirees also mention taxes as a prominent concern. As we age, we become more aware of taxes than when we were young. We have had more experience with government, for one thing. We know how things work, and develop a sense of fairness. We want to pay our share—that is, our fair share. Smart investors come to realize that they must be actively involved in tax planning. You can't control whether taxes rise or fall, but you can have some control over how much of a bite they have on your portfolio. By doing so, you are not dodging taxes. Rather, you are availing yourself of legitimate ways to save under the tax code. With less money going to the government coffers, you can pass on more to family and charity.

Retirees worry, as well, that they will get sick and need to go into a nursing home. Some shrug at the thought and figure it won't happen to them, but others are terrified, particularly if someone in their family has needed extended care. If you do not plan for that major expense, it could wipe out your savings. No need to lose sleep, however. In Chapter 5, I will show you ways to deal with that risk.

What if you face an emergency and suddenly need to tap your nest egg for a major chunk of money? Your car groans to a halt, or the roof begins leaking torrents, or a loved one badly needs your help. How will that affect you? When you were working and had a paycheck, you felt more comfortable taking on debt for such contingencies in life. Will you want to do that now, on a fixed income?

Inflation has long been a major retiree worry and though it ebbed in recent years, most people acknowledge that it is sure to rear again. Things simply will cost more, and you will need an increasing income to pay for them. The inflation rate has been low in an attempt to stabilize and stimulate the economy. What goes down also goes up. Your investments need to have enough of a growth component to ensure that inflation won't erode your savings year by year. Inflation affects older people differently than younger people, and retirees understandably worry about it.

Will you have anything to leave behind to your children, or to charity? This is a concern that becomes increasingly important as people get into their mid-to-late 70s and 80s. Until then, they are focusing on making sure they will have enough for themselves. Once they sense that they will be fine with the assets that they have accumulated, they look to how they might be a help to those around them in their family and in the community. Something is likely to be left behind, and most people would like to decide for themselves what becomes of it, rather than letting the government seize much of it.

YOU ARE NOT ALONE

I have heard, over and over, all of those concerns from people just like you. Rest assured that you are not alone in what you may be feeling. Apprehension is normal as one anticipates a big change. The concerns of the young change with maturity, and now you have this whole new set of concerns. Those concerns are wide ranging, but in one way or another they involve money and the resources you need for the future. What once would have been a setback could be devastating now. By that I mean not only an economic storm but the storms that strike in many lives: the death of a spouse, for example, or divorce. Divorce, unfortunately, isn't uncommon in retirement years as couples struggle to adjust to the huge changes.

"I have heard, over and over, all of those concerns from people just like you. Rest assured that you are not alone in what you may be feeling."

Big and small, these are common scenarios and situations that people face in retirement. They need not derail you if you anticipate them. With a good financial advisor at your side, you can sort it all out together. I use a team approach: If I personally can't address all of a client's concerns, I bring in someone with the expertise needed. I do not have all the answers. When clients have specialized needs, I route them to the right professionals as part of my service to them.

I am interested in doing all that I can to get my clients on the best path to retirement success as they enter this new phase of life, with new rules of engagement at the crescendo and beyond.

CHAPTER 2

Structure: Reviewing the Four Dimensions of Planning

"Do you wish to be great? Then begin by being. Do you desire to construct a vast and lofty fabric? Think first about the foundations of humility. The higher your structure is to be, the deeper must be its foundation."

—Saint Augustine

A s the drummer in a musical ensemble, I play one of the most structural roles. The drummer provides rhythm and form, and if I do not get it right, the song just doesn't work. I have long since learned that people who are transitioning into retirement likewise need structure or it just won't work out well.

Those who are most interested in getting retirement counsel and advice tend to be relatively well educated. They have learned the importance of structure and appreciate what it can do for them. In working with us, they find what they know will work for them.

The "four dimensions" of retirement planning that we reference in the very name of our practice are, again, 1) income planning, 2) risk and fee analysis, 3) a forward-looking tax review, and 4) estate and legacy planning. In those four dimensions, we offer a streamlined process that is unique to our firm. It allows our clients to see clearly not only where they are coming from but also where they are headed on a simple timeline.

Sometimes, people come in with their statements, and to them they seem to be little more than ink on paper. They have developed saving habits, yet that ink on the page is not terribly useful for them. What we try to do is put some structure to this process and whenever possible take all those pieces and assemble the bigger picture. The process allows us to do that.

Here at Fourth Dimension Financial Group, our four dimensional review process is not a linear one. You can go from the first dimension to the third to the second—not necessarily in order. The process depends on the individual, but if you follow it you can expect consistent results.

A TOUR OF THE FOUR

Income Planning

The first dimension—and foundation—of our process is income planning. First we analyze income sources: What income do you have coming in now, and what income will you have coming in during retirement? Then we compare that to the need.

The simplest and most difficult part of retirement planning comes when I ask people this basic question: If you were to retire tomorrow, how much income do you need every month to feel confident that you have enough? When the clients squirm in their seats and finally start guessing, we eventually find a number. We take that income need and we subtract from that any income sources that are guaranteed, such as Social Security payments and pensions, and then we know what we are planning for now. We know what we are seeking in the equation. It is that income gap.

You look at all those income sources and find out if you are using them as effectively as possible. Social Security claiming strategies are part of this, as are pension claiming strategies—and you need to know how to convert the pile of money that you have accumulated into an income that will be sustainable throughout your retirement.

Risk and Fee Analysis

The second dimension includes two elements. We talk a lot about risk. Most people with whom we meet have no idea how much risk they are taking in their investments. To demonstrate, we stress-test the portfolio. If we were to have another 2001, 2008, or 1987 market crash, how much would your portfolio likely lose in percentage and dollar amount? Is that risk acceptable for you in retirement? We will also look at how much your portfolio could gain if we had another late-'90s bull market. We take a closer look at this in Chapter 5 and also in the appendix.

I find that most people are unwilling to focus on growth potential as they stare retirement in the face. They are more focused on how much they might lose. We analyze a variety of situations in great detail so you will know whether your risk comfort level is appropriate.

Along with that, we do a fee analysis. Fees can make a major difference in accounts of similar quality. If one costs less in fees to have it managed, that's more money that stays in your account. That means you have fewer dollars falling through the cracks. We do a detailed analysis of our clients' portfolios and talk about what those fees mean. No, we're not mad at fees. Fees are part of how money is managed. We want to make sure you are getting appropriate value for the fees that you are paying in all of your accounts.

The Forward-Looking Tax Review

The third dimension of our process we like to call the forward-looking tax review. That might sound like confusion in terms, but when you take your tax documents into your tax planner, whether an accountant or CPA, that professional is typically helping you look backward and say, "This happened last year and we'll account for that." That's what determines the amount of taxes that you pay.

In some situations, the tax professional will help you do forward-looking tax planning. To do financial planning without looking ahead to what kind of tax management we can do seems shortsighted. Therefore, in this dimension, we look at what the taxes have been so we can see your likely tax consequences; but we also look for areas where money fell through the cracks because of tax rules you were not aware of. Often a solution can be as simple as repositioning an asset in a different form to reduce the tax impact, which increases the net utility of the money that you have.

Estate and Legacy Planning

The fourth dimension—estate and legacy planning—involves how the money will be handled during your life and after your passing. Will it be protected? Will it go as efficiently as possible to those you care about? We meet some people who want to start their review in the fourth dimension because they want to talk about passing assets on. For the most part, people wait to touch on that dimension in their planning after they feel confident that they have enough to last their lifetimes. Then they will transition into, "Now that we're okay, let's see about making sure other people will be okay."

OUR MOST VALUABLE ASSET

Those are the four distinct dimensions of our planning process by which you can determine whether you would be comfortable retiring. It will help you to get the timing right.

In our physical, 3-D world, beyond the easily measured dimensions of height, width and depth, the fourth dimension is often considered to be time. Time means everything in virtually all aspects of retirement planning, from arranging your income sources to efficiently managing your estate.

As you consider all your choices during financial planning, time is a critical element that determines how to proceed. Time can be our greatest ally, and it can be our greatest detractor as well. We want to maximize the time that we have remaining, free of worry about money so that we can enjoy it. Time is our most valuable asset.

"The fourth dimension is often considered to be time. Time means everything in virtually all aspects of retirement planning, from arranging your income sources to efficiently managing your estate."

In our four dimension review process, the fourth one of estate planning involves not only how you handle your assets in life to make the most of them, but also how they will be handled and distributed after your passing. In other words, that fourth dimension is about time. And it is about time that you considered such matters if you are approaching retirement.

CHAPTER 3

Clarity: Hitting the Right Beat for Your Life Goals

"For me the greatest beauty always lies in the greatest clarity."

—Gotthold Ephraim Lessing

"Clarity affords focus."

—Thomas Leonard

I f I were to ask you to go into the woods and survive for five days on your own, would you rather have a chainsaw or a Swiss Army knife? Most people would say, "I don't know what I'm going to encounter, so probably the Swiss Army knife." Suppose that I asked this instead: "If I send you into the woods to cut down the biggest tree as soon as possible, which would you rather have?" Clearly you would want the chainsaw.

In retirement planning, your job as the client is to explain what you are trying to accomplish, and I will find the right tools for that. First, I need to get to know you. Often, when new clients come in with a pile of statements, they want to dive right in. "If it is okay," I tell them, "let me get to know you before I get to know your assets."

Money is the means to an end. It means something different to everybody. Money can mean power, status, and independence, but ultimately it is a tool that can get you your end results. You just want to make sure that you know what those end results are.

My job, as I see it, is first to help you get a better view of your long-distance targets. Perhaps I will need to help you identify them and then get them into focus. To the extent that you can see the target more clearly, you are more likely to hit the bulls-eye. I aim to draw out of people what's most important to them about money— that is, what's most important to them about the use of the money as a tool. Getting that clarity is critical.

Think of the huge impact that a conductor, director, or bandleader can have on the music. Everybody can know his or her part but still needs someone to stand up there to say, "Here is what we are looking for. Let me define it. Let me describe it to you. Here's what I want it to feel like. Here's what I want it to do to our audience." The best conductors I have ever worked with are those who are abundantly clear about what they are trying to create. That allows the musicians to step back and have a much clearer sense of their role in creating that final picture. That is where we hit this balance. I need people to tell me what they want, and my job is to help them get it.

It is a fun part of the retirement planning process. It's when people really start to think. "What do I really want my life to be about?" they ask themselves. "What have I always wanted to do but never had time to do it, or never had the freedom because I was always caring for others? What do I want to do before my time is up?" It is a wonderful time to dream. You need to do that, and then we will look for ways to connect the dollars to those outcomes.

If somebody comes in with a number of accounts, I will ask: "What is the purpose of this money? What's the reason for this account?" They often reply, in effect, "I don't know." I suggest to them that we dig deeper because when I understand how they want to use the money, I can give them the most efficient strategy, tools, and products to do that.

One of the questions that help the most in clarifying your financial goals is this: How do you want to be remembered? When people consider what they want their legacy to be, they begin to see that their money and assets can be a means to that end.

"One of the questions that help the most in clarifying your financial goals is this: How do you want to be remembered?"

YOUR EARLIEST MEMORY OF MONEY

We do not talk about money as much as we should. We do not always understand our innermost motivations. In working with clients, sometimes I have to take them back to their early impressions in life to get a perspective that will allow me to prescribe a financial solution. This is a question that I learned from Mitch Anthony, a renowned advisor to financial services professionals. I'll ask: "Think back as far as you can and tell me your first recollection of money."

I have heard stories about striping baseball diamonds as a 12-year-old. I have heard paper route stories. I have heard, "This is how my dad responded when I asked for money when I was eight." Sometimes it is not the earliest memory, but it is a profound one. It is the first one that comes to mind.

Many years later that story that people tell themselves still has a huge impact on how they manage their money. It can be a barrier in their decision to retire and leave paid work. By getting very clear about what money means to you and what the purpose is and what those goals are, you can get on course to a fulfilling retirement.

I have had some of the biggest breakthroughs in our meetings when I have asked that question. Gaining that perspective gives you a sense of purpose in how you deal with money. And it helps couples work in concert toward their common goals. I have found that often, a husband and wife do not really know each other's innermost feelings about money and what drives the other spouse's decisions. They do not think to tell each other those early money stories. They do not think to ask. When they do recall a money memory, they might feel at first that it has little significance, yet it turns out that the experience has impacted every financial decision they made in the last 40 or 50 years.

When I work with couples, I find that one spouse is often quite different from the other. One fears loss; one pushes for gain. My challenge is to show that protection and growth both have their place, within reason. In retirement, part of your accumulated portfolio must be guaranteed against loss. You will need that money, and losing it would be devastating. You also, however, need to temper that caution by pursuing the opportunity to grow another part of your portfolio. That's how you counter inflation, and that's how you enhance your lifestyle.

I seek to understand each spouse's needs and to serve them as a couple. One may have received an inheritance and a free ride in college; the other may have worked through school. We have to find that balance, and that is why we often have to arrive at the "his" and "hers" plan. Along the way, I can best help people when they are willing to dig deep and find out what money truly means to them.

"I can best help people when they are willing to dig deep and find out what money truly means to them."

WHAT WILL MAKE YOU HAPPY?

The only reason that you would want to retire from paid work is because something is more important to you. Otherwise it is ingrained in us to continue to work for money. We need money. It is a wellspring for survival and power. That's why the paycheck matters so much to us, and the only reason we stop working is for the pursuit of joy in other areas of life. As we work together in retirement planning, we want to find out what makes you happy. What is on your list?

A question I love to ask is this: "In three years, what will have to have happened financially for you to feel really happy with your progress?" As my client, you sit there and think, and then you start to tell me what's important to you. We are looking ahead and finding out what would really make you happy. What would make you feel safe or successful? We'll begin to turn those feelings into tangible outcomes.

Most people want to spend more time with family, and we can certainly support that desire by helping them figure out how to spend three months a year down in Texas seeing the grandkids, or the best way to get the family together once a year for a vacation in Myrtle Beach. Many also want to travel, particularly in the first several years of retirement. Other goals are unique to the individual or the couple, and once they identify their heart's desires, I can help to connect the dots financially.

Those goals also will include whether and how to pass on wealth. There too I often find differences of opinion between husband and wife. The wife, for example, may want to help the grandkids now, while the husband may want to help them, yes, but with whatever is left. That's a generalization, of course, but my point is that it is common for spouses to need to talk through their goals and come to terms with how they will pursue them. I am not looking to see what makes one of them happy while leaving the other discouraged. This is a time for close communication.

BE REALISTIC

The goals, once identified, must be realistic. It all starts with determining how much money you need each month for essential expenses and assessing how much remains for discretionary expenses. Once you do that, you quickly will be able to see whether the goals you have stated are attainable, given the resources available. If they are not, the solution might be to work an additional year or two, which can be a major boost financially. If indeed you are heading toward something that you deem exciting, then you will work joyfully that last year in anticipation of it.

It is a matter of organizing your life and gaining clarity about what you want in the years ahead. From there, we can take a look at the documents of your financial life and chart your course. We ask clients to gather those, and we organize them into a binder. Sometimes clients groan when they see the list of what to bring to those early meetings —account statements, insurance policies, estate documents, pension plans, tax forms, for example—but in gathering those, you are getting a grip on your financial state of affairs.

"It is a matter of organizing your life and gaining clarity about what you want in the years ahead. From there, we can take a look at the documents of your financial life and chart your course."

That organizing, in itself, helps you to find the clarity that you will need as you identify your life goals. It helps us to broaden the conversation and see all the possibilities. If the dreams expressed do not match the resources available, we will see that discrepancy early enough to find a way to bring them into alignment.

WHO SHOULD KNOW?

Clients sometimes wonder how close to hold their cards. Who should know about their financial affairs? Should the children be privy to their finances and assets? Couples differ in their feelings about that, but generally they want to share some things but not everything. Or not with everyone. In many families, one of the children is not as financially responsible as the others, and that can create conflict.

Some clients are interested in such multigenerational planning, reasoning that the more information they share, the better their heirs will be able to manage their inheritance and plan for themselves. Other clients decide it is best not to reveal much. It's entirely a matter of preference. You are the best judge of your family dynamics.

In either case, you will want to consider how much trust you can place in those who will one day manage what you leave to them. There is no escaping the fact that the day may come when you will be unable to manage your own finances. For many people, the sooner they can involve an executor or family member, the better. As we set our goals for a lifetime and beyond, these will be the people who see to our affairs for the long term and who can help to establish our legacy.

CHAPTER 4

Harmony: Performing in Perfect Tune with Others

"Harmony makes small things grow; lack
of it makes great things decay."

—Sallust

We are awash in information. It can feel as if we are drowning in it at times, and the volume is bound to increase. With so many people to listen to, and so many sites to surf, just who can you trust? Who should get your attention?

As you approach retirement, such discernment is critical. Everyone seems to have a competing view, and it can be hard to know where to turn. We know that it is important to begin the planning early, but it is just as important to go to the right sources.

For any advice that you receive, you must put it in context. Where did it come from, and what was the expectation of how that advice or information would be used? There are a number of players in the financial advice game. Let's take a look at a few of those.

GRAINS OF SALT

As people near retirement, they also are nearing the end of the accumulation phase of their lives, and it is likely that for decades stockbrokers played a huge role in that phase. Stockbrokers help people find risk-based assets so that in theory they can better accumulate wealth, but generally the focus is not on protection. When the economy and your portfolio take a dip, the stockbrokers try to console you by telling you that the market will come back in time. They suggest that time will fix everything.

FIDUCIARY VERSUS SUITABILITY

In trying to sort through it all, most people will see the wisdom of seeking the counsel of a financial advisor. You will want to look at the advisor's background and expertise, and you will want to ask how the advisor has deepened his or her knowledge in that specialty.

I chose to pursue the designation of Retirement Income Certified Professional®, or RICP®, because it is so on-topic for our clientele. There are a lot of designations, so I encourage people to research what they mean and whether that designation will serve their particular planning needs.

It is also important when choosing an advisor to assess whatever biases he/she might be bringing to the table. Everyone seeking advice should understand these two terms: *fiduciary* and *suitability*. What does it mean to be a fiduciary? What is the suitability standard for your investments?

A fiduciary is essentially someone who acts in the best interest of another, as a caretaker of that person's finances. In giving advice, the fiduciary's own interest must not be at the forefront. A fiduciary is required to do what's best for the client.

The standard of suitability, by contrast, can just mean this: Is the investment good enough? The suitability model is the one by which the vast majority of financial representatives, including broker/dealers, operate. Most of the big-name financial houses fall within the suitability category. See the appendix for more.

In the first five years of my career, I experienced that world. It is a world in which the agent represents a firm that offers products and services. Firms offer them through a distribution network of advisors. Typically, the firm sells its own branded products and services, or a very narrow scope of offerings. Under such a system, you have to wonder whether the "best" product for every client just happens to be one that the company offers. Clearly, that's not necessarily the case; the product is merely suitable in some fashion.

By contrast, a fiduciary advisor is set up to offer products and services from a variety of money managers, insurance companies and financial service providers so that they can present those that are in the client's best interest. They are not restricted to some firm's proprietary offerings.

It is an important distinction: Are you working with a fiduciary who must serve your best interest, or are you working with a sales rep whose primary interest is that of the companies he/she represents? What is "suitable" really comes down to the question of whether it could harm the client. The standard is much lower than it is for the fiduciary model, in which the advisor must show due diligence in seeking the best product and solution.

"It is an important distinction: Are you working with a fiduciary who must serve your best interest, or are you working with a sales rep whose primary interest is that of the companies he/she represents?"

WHO'S ON YOUR SIDE?

How do you know which kind of specialist you are dealing with? Can you tell by the credentials or the initials after the name whether you are dealing with a fiduciary? Can you do some research on a prospective advisor to learn his or her standards? Those questions do not necessarily have easy answers.

Typically, a fiduciary advisor will be from a firm with the RIA (Registered Investment Advisor) designation. That advisor will have to share with you firm documents in the form of an ADV Part 2A, an ADV Part 2B. Those are the disclosures that fiduciary advisors are required to offer prospective and current clients. They lay out their fee structure, the firm's practices, and disclose any conflicts of interest. By contrast, somebody operating in the suitability world is not required to share any conflicts of interest, their fee arrangements, or their firm's practices. Generally, if you ask them for their ADV documents, they will look blankly at you. They do not know what those are, because they are not required to furnish them. I have to give a copy of those ADVs to my clients whether they ask for them or not. They will sign that they have received them as part of the planning and advisory agreement with an RIA firm.

A major battle has been going on in the industry and has been made more public by the passage of the Dodd-Frank Act, legislation aimed at financial industry reform and consumer protection. The goal is for the industry to operate under one fiduciary standard, but many of the big broker/dealers are fighting it and with a ferocity that makes one wonder why they are so against it. In short, their revenue model depends on a lot of hidden costs and hidden revenue streams.

Those who are not fiduciaries will often tell clients that they are. Saying so doesn't make it so. The client needs to understand what really makes that distinction. In the end, a fiduciary is likely from an RIA firm, as opposed to a registered representative advisor of a broker/dealer. I am not out to slam the wire houses. The great majority of advisors started out in a captive agent model, in which they were under the suitability guidelines. But with time and experience, many advisors begin to question that system and desire instead to move toward an arrangement that truly is best for the client. I did so at great financial cost, and I think it is where the industry is ultimately heading.

FEES AND COMMISSIONS

Some advisors are fee based, and some are commission based. On the investment side, we are a fee-only advisor, meaning we do not earn commissions. We do earn commissions on insurance-based products, not because we prefer it that way but because that is how those products are designed. Because my firm specializes in retirement planning, many clients want and need products that guarantee protection against risks such as longevity, premature death and long-term-care needs. All of those products are insurance based. You cannot get guarantees from a mutual fund or stock companies. We disclose that to clients in our ADVs. A broker/dealer who earns commissions on mutual funds and insurance products generally doesn't tell you that.

BUILDING RAPPORT AND TRUST

In weighing all those considerations, it comes down to this: Does the advisor really know you and care about you? Without that human connection, you are unlikely to be satisfied with how your money is handled. Money is the means to an end: to create the life you envision. Without a shared vision you are likely to feel misdirected on that journey.

That's why it is important to develop the type of relationship in which your advisor can ask you specific and personal questions so that he/she can make financial recommendations in your best interest. Trust your instincts. An advisor who serves up recommendations too quickly may care more about your assets than about you. Certainly, be wary of any advisor who shies away from your questions. Try to get to know the advisor well enough to sense whether you would enjoy working together, because, after all, you will be spending hours together making sure your planning is on track. Ask your friends whether they like their advisors. Such referrals can help immensely.

We encourage people to meet quarterly with us. That regular contact is important to adjusting to lifestyle change, particularly the transition into retirement. Once our clients feel reassured that the plan is working, they often feel less need for regular contact, and yet it still is important to stay in touch. We set up regular quarterly events for our clients. They are social gatherings, but we offer economic updates and opportunities aplenty to reconnect with us. We value the person behind the statements, and we want a relationship.

YOU NEED A COACH AND A TEAM

Good advisors will not dodge your questions because they understand where you are coming from and know the nuances. Such an advisor is like a coach. In sports, an athlete cannot reach the greatest heights without a coach. You might think that the very best athletes would not need coaches, but they still hire them. You'll rarely see a top-level tennis player out at Wimbledon without a coach nearby, evaluating the performance and offering feedback.

With a financial advisor who is on your side, you gain the advantage of accountability. You have somebody who is in that world all day every day and can synthesize all that information out there and present it to you in a way that makes sense. That's why it is so important to find an advisor you like to work with and can trust.

One sign that you have found a good one is when you see your advisor regularly offering to bring other professional advice givers into the relationship. The amount of information that's out there can be daunting not only for the client but for the advisor as well. A well-structured plan has an emphasis on tax efficiency. It needs legal assurances and controls. It protects against catastrophes. That is why, with the client's permission, we can introduce tax counsel and CPAs. We can bring an estate planning attorney into the relationship, and independent insurance agents. If the client already has such relationships, we are willing to interact with those people. The goal is to make sure we have a holistic plan.

"One sign that you have found a good one is when you see your advisor regularly offering to bring other professional advice givers into the relationship."

If the advisor doesn't offer such relationships or shies away from such contacts, it is understandable that you will be left wondering what that advisor is hiding. What is he/she afraid of? Will the plan he recommends stand up to the light of day? Are there flaws she doesn't want other professionals to see? We find that we serve our clients better with a team approach, integrating our services with those of other professionals.

An athlete might need a strength coach, cardio coach, a dietary coach, mental toughness coach. You do not generally get one coach if you are a top level athlete, and I do not think you should have just one coach when your goal is to not run out of money before you pass away. That's a big deal. You need advice you can trust.

In the appendix you will find "Sure-Fire Steps to Hiring the Right Advisor" to help you better understand what to look for when seeking the right advisor for you and your needs.

CHAPTER 5

Consonance, Dissonance: Avoiding Unpleasant Passages

"If you ask what is the single most important key to longevity,
I would have to say it is avoiding worry, stress and tension.
And if you didn't ask me, I'd still have to say it."

—George Burns

"**A**dam, help us to get our money back." That was the simple plea that I heard from a couple who came in for a visit in March 2009, after the recession had taken its toll. I had never met them before, but their predicament was all too familiar. They had been retired for a couple of years and wanted to talk about what had happened to the portfolio they were depending upon to see them through.

They looked at each other and then at me. With tears streaming down his face, the husband declared to his wife that he had blown it. He had been proud about managing his own investments, and now, their account was worth half of what it had been before the crash. He knew his wife had trusted him and he felt the full burden of the loss. They felt devastated.

That was a story that I am sure played out all over the country. Still, it is hard for an advisor to hear about such situations. Even without knowing them, I knew their anguish. I feel a sense of responsibility to help anyone who crosses my path, and I wanted to help that couple arrive at a better place. But there is only so much you can do when a portfolio has lost half its value. They had been out of work by choice for several years and didn't know where to turn.

That scenario can be avoided. It is not that people do not recognize the danger of what could happen. The RICP program cites 27 risks that a retiree faces, which I have listed in the appendix to this book. Retirees' foremost concern is: "What if I run out of money?" In fact, in an AARP poll from 2010, 61 percent of the 3,000 people surveyed, ages 44 to 75, replied that they feared running out of money more than they feared death itself.

How can you gain some assurance that your money will last as long as you do? A good first step is to get a clear understanding of just what those risks are that could threaten your portfolios. Once we have identified those risks, we can subject your portfolio to stress testing so that you can see how you will be doing, come what may. Later in this chapter, I will explain more about this important and intriguing aspect of retirement planning.

Let's take a closer look now at those risks you face in retirement. Some of them you will see mentioned in various contexts throughout this book, but for perspective let's look at several of them here.

Longevity Risk

A major one is simply longevity risk, and that's really what those in the survey were addressing. People are living longer. Will the money last? The statistics are daunting. So many forces can eat away at a portfolio, and the risks that we will examine now all play into that fundamental one of longevity. After all, if people lived, on average, only a few years into retirement, as they typically did a century ago, many of these issues would be moot.

"If people lived, on average, only a few years into retirement, as they typically did a century ago, many of these issues would be moot."

Inflation Risk

Inflation is a major issue, and people need to consider it carefully now in the wake of years of government efforts to stimulate the economy. It should come as no surprise that in the future things will cost more than they do now. Every year the government publishes the inflation rate, but we need to remember that inflation is different for everyone. Retirees will experience a different rate than, say, a young married couple setting up a household. People with different needs spend money on different things. In retirement planning we need to structure inflation risk into the portfolio in recognition of those expenses that you are most likely to face.

The brokers and those who are in the stock market model of investment will commonly say that market-based investments typically do really well as a hedge against inflation. Words such as "typically" or "often" can get a little scary for people who are facing retirement. If you look at Japan as an example, its stock market crashed and has not recovered even in the face of significant long-term inflation, demonstrating that stock market investments are not guaranteed to rise with inflation. We want to build inflation-fighting investments and instruments into your retirement and income plan so that you can keep pace with inflation.

For retirees, one of the biggest inflationary items will be medical costs. Inflation could become a major risk for general medical care, long-term care, a nursing home stay, or acute care at home. As most people move further into retirement, they spend less on gasoline and air fares. They drive less and go on fewer vacations. But as those expenses go down, retirees tend to need more medical care. That expense rises, and inflation pushes it even higher. We need to make sure that those costs are factored into your plan.

"For retirees, one of the biggest inflationary items will be medical costs."

Market Risk

It seems that about every five to eight years the market has a major "correction" or a crash. Nonetheless, most investors during their accumulation years take the advice that you need to accept risk to make money. They therefore invest in stocks or mutual funds that own stocks. Bonds now present significant risks as well because of the very low interest rate environment that we are in.

The brokers and the accumulation specialists who advise you to take risk do not often recognize the range of factors that can deplete a retiree's portfolio. A recent DALBAR study on the real performance of the market over the last 20 years found that the typical investor in the market had a return far less than the 8 percent range cited for the market performance in general. Equity investors ended up with a 4.25 percent return, while those investing in a stock/bond mix had a 2.29 percent return. A 20-year horizon is fine for investors in the accumulation phase of their financial lives, but a retiree can't afford a downturn in those 20 years. Market risk can have a disastrous effect on a retiree, especially if the losses come early in retirement.

The stockbrokers will tell you that simply allocating your assets in a mixture of stocks and bonds is a way to diversify it. Then when your portfolio does go down, you generally will hear this when you call that broker: "Well the market goes up; it goes down, but just hang in there; it'll come back." That does not bring a lot of comfort to a retiree.

When there's no paycheck to replace those losses, the do-overs are difficult. The broker, typically, gets paid either way, whether the portfolio goes up or down. Because brokers are paid by commissions on trades, their incentives are not necessarily aligned with the investor's interests. A major correction can devastate retirees who must continue to live on their life's savings.

Think of it this way: If you worked 35 years to accumulate a million dollars, a 20 percent loss in your portfolio value would wipe out what amounts to a fifth of those years of savings. That's seven years of lost savings. Even a 1 percent decline in the market would cost you about four months.

"Think of it this way: If you worked 35 years to accumulate a million dollars, a 20 percent loss in your portfolio value would wipe out what amounts to a fifth of those years of savings."

The deeper the hit that a portfolio takes, the greater the return needed for its recovery. That pain is particularly acute for the retiree who has ceased adding new income and investment to that account. When the retiree instead is withdrawing money at the same time that the market is pummeling the account, the effect is devastating.

That in fact is the greatest risk, aside, possibly, from the costs of long-term care that can deplete a retiree's portfolio. That's what happened to that couple who came to me in March 2009, having lost half the value of their nest egg. Their choices were few. They could go back to work, but they already had been retired for a number of years. They could cut way back on spending. Or they could hope beyond

hope that the money would reappear. Those are tough choices. For-
tunately, much can be done to prevent such a scenario.

The markets have been highly volatile, and volatility wreaks
havoc on retirees' portfolios when they are taking money out for
their income. Once it was believed that the best strategy to protect
yourself was to just diversify your investments. The rationale was that
if you put the right percentage in stocks and the right percentage
in bonds, your portfolio would be safe if the market declined. In
other words, the safety of bonds would prop up your portfolio if the
market declined. If the market rose, then certainly you would make
less in the bond part of the portfolio but you would make more on
the stock portfolio.

Today's concern regarding bonds is that we are in an interest rate
environment that's the lowest in recorded history. Bond prices are
inversely related to interest rates. As rates rise, the bond prices fall.
Let's say you bought a bond for $1,000 that pays 3 percent. If in a
few years people will be able to buy a bond that pays 6 percent, will
they be interested in yours? No, because it would be worth increasingly less as rates continued to rise in the market as a whole.

Investors had been flocking to bonds to gain more safety in their
portfolio and become more diversified, but that bond bubble is likely
to burst when interest rates in the prevailing market rise. Achieving
safety is not as easy as it once sounded in these days of a highly
volatile stock market and of a bond market under the pressure that
rates likely will rise.

True diversification requires more than simply a mix of stocks
and bonds. True diversification for retirees includes product diversification. That includes having a portion of your retirement portfolio in

guaranteed investments that protect against living too long, market declines, or bond losses that result from rising interest rates.

It is a different outlook. Most brokers and advisors who are of the accumulation mindset are simply not looking at it that way. They are often unprepared and lack access to the best products and solutions to give true diversification to retirees. That's why we specialize. The body of knowledge needed to protect retirees is so extensive that you need to work with a specialist.

Tax Risk

When I speak to audiences, I'll ask: "By a show of hands, how many in the room think that taxes will go down in the future?" Not a single hand goes up. In fact, people start laughing. "How many people think taxes will be the same in the future?" More laughter. Obviously people are concerned that taxes are going to go up in the future.

We have been in a relatively low tax environment by historical standards. However, the government bailout of large companies and the economy will have to be paid back somehow. That could be one indication that higher taxes are on the way, a significant risk for retirees. If the government has a greater stake in your retirement assets, that means you will have less to spend. Not only are you fighting forces such as inflation and market risk but you also are hampered by higher tax rates. Taxation is a significant drain on your spending and purchasing power in retirement.

Let me give you a sense of what I mean by that. In all those years of saving and accumulating, the prevailing wisdom was that you should defer as much tax as possible. Max out your 401(k) or the 403(b) retirement plan or your deductible IRA, people were told, and worry about taxes by deferring them into the future. It was beaten into their heads that they could grow their money faster if they did not have the burden of taxes right away.

But there's a day of reckoning that comes when you have to take the money out of those tax-deferred accounts. You actually are likely to face higher taxation at a time when you believed you would be in a lower tax bracket. Higher tax rates have put you in harm's way when it comes to tax efficiency. People who believed they would move into a very low tax bracket are paying higher income taxes in retirement. In some cases, 15 to 25 percent of that 401(k) is not yours. The government has laid claim to it with higher taxes.

"There's a day of reckoning that comes when you have to take the money out of those tax-deferred accounts. You actually are likely to face higher taxation at a time when you believed you would be in a lower tax bracket."

It is a huge mistake to continue to defer all those accounts without an eye on how to create efficient income distribution strategies during retirement. There are ways to make your income stream more tax efficient.

Another reason that a lot of people believe taxes will go up is that trillions of tax-deferred dollars are in those retirement plans and the government will be looking for ways to pay off debt. Why not raise taxes to tap the money in those retirement plans? It is a reality we must face. It makes sense to seek out an advisor who can help work with your tax professionals to create a tax-efficient income.

The traditional retirement plan was a pension funded by your employer. That pension created a guaranteed paycheck for life. It was a bedrock of financial security for families. The days of pensions are nearly gone, and countless families have felt the threat to their security. To replace that loss, people have been forced to do their own research and planning to build what amounts to their own pension plan.

The 401(k) and 403(b) retirement plans that have largely replaced pensions have fallen short for many people. Many have not funded their employer plan to the same level that their pensions were funded. They are arriving at retirement with less money, and lacking expertise in how to build a portfolio. The risks in the market and the volatility have shaken that financial bedrock. The 401(k) has created a lot of moving pieces for people who just were good at their jobs and didn't want the second job of managing a retirement portfolio. The 401(k) has its merits, but it has some real flaws that people need to reckon with.

One strategy that could make sense for certain clients is to convert part of their traditional IRAs, or their 401(k)s that become IRAs, into a Roth IRA. The Roth IRA conversion sounds really attractive. It allows a retiree, or anyone for that matter, to take part or all of their IRA, convert it to a Roth, and pay the taxes now on the amount converted. That way they are not deferring taxes into a higher tax rate in the future. They are paying the tax today, and they can use the money tax free during their retirement. Mathematically, it makes wonderful sense if we assume that tax rates are going to go up. A lot of people should consider converting a portion or perhaps all of their IRA assets.

When people do consider a Roth conversion, however, what happens in my experience is that they see the tax bill they'll have to pay and they simply can't get themselves to commit. The conversion is considered a withdrawal from their IRA and that added income pushes them into a much higher tax bracket. Moreover, they have to pay that tax out of funds that are not part of the IRA being converted. Many people just can't get themselves to pursue what might be a good move for them.

Alternatively, we can build an income strategy in which clients use some tax-deferred money from IRAs or 401(k)s in combination with some taxable assets. The goal is to maximize the income available to them in the lowest possible tax bracket by blending taxable and nontaxable assets. I enjoy helping clients with that strategy. Once they see how it works, they recognize that it is a balanced approach that avoids the pain of a large Roth IRA conversion.

Risk of High Fees

Investors cannot control a lot of things, but they certainly can find ways to pay less in fees. By doing some research, an investor can seek out lower fee alternatives. Mutual funds, which are the investment of choice for a great many people, are getting a lot of negative press for the amount of hidden fees and costs within them.

Studies have shown that the average mutual fund has a fee exposure of over 3 percent per year. You may be thinking that sounds ludicrous, particularly since the prospectus for your mutual fund— which I'm sure you have read cover to cover—probably shows the typical ratio of 1 percent to 1.5 percent. But regulations currently do not require many of the costs and fees inside those accounts to be fully disclosed in the prospectus.

"Studies have shown that the average mutual fund has a fee exposure of over 3 percent per year."

The fees come in the form of transaction costs; turnover costs; legal costs; and 12b-1 fees, which you pay the mutual fund family to advertise that fund to you and others. If two investments are of equal merit but one has higher fees, you have to ask yourself whether it would behoove you to go with the lower fee investment so that less is drained from your account.

We hear a lot about the beauty of compound interest, but we do not often hear about the tyranny of compounding fees. Over time, fees can have a huge effect. They amount to a huge risk for people who are trying to keep more money in their pocket. Fees can significantly reduce the longevity of a portfolio for a retiree.

"We hear a lot about the beauty of compound interest, but we do not often hear about the tyranny of compounding fees."

It is sort of the reverse of the way that compound interest can magically and wonderfully increase by many times the value of your account when you are contributing. As those fees continue to tap the value of your return, you lose the benefit of that compounding. They amount to a hidden tax that goes undisclosed.

A fiduciary advisor, an RIA, is required to disclose all of the fees. Our new clients often are surprised the first time they see the statement in their institutional investment account. They see every transaction, including every fee charged. That is a very different experience than when you own the XYZ growth fund, for example, and do not see the fees. Ultimately, the hidden fees create a drag on the returns in your account. Meanwhile if the market is falling and taxes are rising and you are withdrawing income from your account, you have a major problem.

However, by effectively exercising control over your market risk, fees and asset allocation, you can arrive at a retirement plan that will work for you. That control starts with awareness and many people simply are unaware of the extent to which fees could be setting them back.

Health-Care Risk

There's no question that one of the major risks that people face is a health-care crisis that could deplete a portfolio rapidly. In my state, Ohio, for example, the annual cost of a nursing-home stay currently is between $74,000 and $82,000 per year. If one spouse's long-term care costs that much, the other spouse's lifestyle could be in serious jeopardy.

This, understandably, is one of the major concerns among retirees, and it is a risk that needs to be managed. People are more open to talking about it when they near retirement because often they have had a personal experience—usually a family member who needed care—that woke them up to the reality of how much it costs.

Still, some people continue to believe that they do not need to plan for long-term care because Medicare and Medicaid will pay for it. That's not true. Medicare is not designed to pay for nursing home costs and pays very little toward them. Medicaid essentially requires that you first become poor before it will kick in and pay for the costs of long-term care. Regulations vary by state, but generally people have to spend down their assets until little remains. The spouse at home can keep the house, wedding ring, and a small amount of money. In order for Medicaid to foot the bill, you have to have depleted all your other assets. That's a difficult scenario for retirees and their families, particularly when they could have protected against it.

Some long-term-care assistance is available to veterans, but again the requirement generally is that they have few assets. There are other alternatives, but it comes down to this: The need for long-term care is a significant risk for retirees, and you need to start planning well in advance so that you are prepared.

In the past it was common for people to make themselves indigent on paper by transferring assets so that they would qualify for Medicaid coverage. For example, a mother would transfer all of her money to her children. The "look-back" period was three years. If that amount of time had passed and mom now needed care, she qualified because she had no money of her own. Today the look-back period is five years, and there are other rules on giving money away.

Transferring your money can present significant risks. Let's say that Mom gets the money out of her estate by giving it to the kids.

Then one or more of the kids faces a creditor issue, loses a job, goes through a divorce, or faces a lawsuit, or the money is in some way mismanaged. The money is gone. Mom still needs long-term care but she has no access to that money.

There are ways that an estate planning attorney can structure a plan to prepare a family for the need for long-term care. To make yourself poor on paper by simply giving the money to the kids is very dangerous. There are better ways to plan.

"There are ways that an estate planning attorney can structure a plan to prepare a family for the need for long-term care. To make yourself poor on paper by simply giving the money to the kids is very dangerous."

LONG-TERM-CARE PLANNING OPTIONS

Let's take a look at some of the options for funding long-term care, should the need arise—and this particular risk is so significant that you will want to consider these options carefully.

There are four distinct options: 1) self-pay, 2) traditional long-term-care insurance, 3) life insurance with care benefits, and 4) an annuity with care benefits.

The self-pay option is just what it sounds like: If you determine that you have enough assets to shoulder the risk, you may decide to pay for long-term care out of pocket if the need arises. One way to determine whether to maintain or to transfer this risk is to ask yourself if the full cost of a lengthy care need would affect your ability to meet your other financial goals for spousal income and/or gifting. If you're not sure, you may want to consider transferring at least some of the risk to an insurance company.

With the second option, long-term-care insurance, you pay premiums on a policy monthly or annually for years as protection against the possibility of a long-term-care need. You basically are purchasing a set amount of monthly benefits to be payable to the long-term-care facility or caregiver. Those monthly benefits are payable over a predetermined number of years or up to a total amount of pooled benefits paid out. At death, the benefits cease.

The downside of that is some insurance companies have dropped out of the market because the costs of care have gone up so much. Premiums have gone up a significant amount over the last number of years with some of the big carriers. And some people feel uncomfortable that if they never need long-term care, they will have "lost" the money that they paid in premiums. If you could know that you would need long-term care in a nursing home, traditional long-term-care insurance could be the most efficient and powerful way to fund the care. But nobody has a crystal ball.

The third and fourth options have become possible as a result of the Pension Protection Act of 2006. One of those is a life-insurance-linked long-term-care solution. Basically, that is a life insurance policy with long-term-care benefits attached to it. There are a number of different versions of this. They come under different names. The critical feature here is you buy a life insurance policy with that long-term-care provision added, often in the form of a rider.

If long-term care is needed, you are essentially spending the death benefit during your life for the long-term-care need. Any money left over gets passed to the beneficiary on the policy as a life insurance death benefit. If no long-term care was needed, it simply remains a life insurance policy and the death benefit passes on in a tax-free manner to the beneficiary on the policy.

Those policies are interesting because you have a return of premium provision. Let's say that long-term care isn't needed, the life insurance policy isn't wanted, and the policy holder just wants to get the money back. The policy holder can get the money and premiums back from the policy during his or her life. It is the first time you've really had a way to not have a "use it or lose it" scenario. That's becoming a much more popular option.

The other option made possible under the Pension Protection Act is an annuity that has long-term-care benefits linked to it as well. Basically, you fund an annuity, typically, with a lump sum of money. If you need the income from the annuity, that's what it is designed for. In the event of a long-term-care need, that annuity will pay additional money in the form of a home-health-care doubler during that period of care, generally up to about five years. Should the person who needs the care pass away, a lifetime income generally will continue for the joint owner or joint annuitant for the rest of their life.

In summary, long-term-care insurance can be a reliable way to insure against a very significant risk, but whether it is affordable or not depends on your situation. For people with fewer assets, at least some of the risk might be covered by the new options of life-insurance-linked and annuity-linked benefits. Such products can serve the dual purpose of providing an income and funding long-term care if necessary.

STRESS TESTING YOUR PLAN

Those, then, are several of the primary risks that retirees face: inflation, the volatile market, taxes, fees, the cost of care. There are numerous others, as listed in the appendix. When we are putting together a retirement and income plan, we want to address of many of those risks as possible.

Once we draw out an entire plan and put all the appropriate pieces in place, I ask my clients to go down the list of all their concerns. I ask them to review all of those 27 risks of retirement that we identified, and all the concerns that might keep them up at night. Then we look at how the plan would respond to those risks. What happens if we return to high inflation? What happens if there's a long-term-care need? If the market crashes, what happens to the plan?

I sketch out the plan on a smartboard, and the client and I take shots at it as we continue with the stress testing: We subject it to real-world forces and tweak it until the client's fears and concerns are satisfied. The objective is to mitigate or transfer as much risk as possible. Stress-testing the plan is a highly effective way to ensure that you are not just hoping all goes well but that you are planning for a wonderful and sustainable retirement even in light of those potential risks.

Stress-testing the plan is a highly effective way to ensure that you are not just hoping all goes well

One specific measure we take to stress-test a plan is to quantify the risk present in the current investment portfolio. In the appendix you will see a specific example of this that will help you better understand how critical this is for a retiree. Without understanding how a portfolio will respond to a market crash, retirees are at great risk of mismanaging their assets. The technology is available, so it is highly encouraged to learn the true nature of how a portfolio will perform when market values fall.

Asking what-ifs is a must. That's when we know we have a rock-solid income plan. "Man, you've got an answer for everything," a client joked as we stress-tested his plan. I said, "Well, what's most important is that your plan does, because we designed it that way."

Rhythm: Finding the Right Timing for a Reliable Income

"I learned that we can do anything, but we can't do everything—at least not at the same time. So think of your priorities not in terms of what activities you do but when you do them. Timing is everything."

—Dan Millman

I have pictures in my office of my six daughters. I agree with the observation that many people make when they see those pictures, or when they meet the girls: They all look the same. They are all blond-haired and blue-eyed; they are just different heights.

But though they look alike and have the same mom and dad, their personalities are quite different. Each has her own qualities and attributes. And that's just the way they are. None of those attributes are inherently good or bad. They simply define unique human beings.

The same is true with financial products. They are not good or bad per se. I like to say financial products are amoral. They just sit on a shelf and wait for you to use them. Their effectiveness is determined by how you use them in your planning.

That is a critical point to understand as we are looking to fund the various components of an income plan. Products that are designed for growth should be used for potential growth. Products that are designed for income should be used for income.

That's where people get confused. They might say, for example, "I heard annuities are bad." And they do often get a bad rap because they are compared unfairly to growth investments. They are not designed for that. They are designed for preservation and income. Some retirees love Certificates of Deposit for their liquidity and safety, but they get upset because of the strings attached, namely, low interest rates. Whatever the financial vehicle, it needs to be put to proper use. If guaranteed and safe investments are used for their best attributes, the growth investments can do their best work, too.

"Whatever the financial vehicle, it
needs to be put to proper use."

They're just different, with different strengths. So it is with people, and so it is with investment tools. Any parent sees the truth in that. If I needed a paper to be proofread, I'd give it to my firstborn because she's a rule follower, and she would make sure I followed the rules too. If I wanted to plan a party, I would go to my middle child who loves to plan fun activities. Each does different things well and deserves recognition for her best attributes. Each also is less skilled at things that one of her sisters might do better.

The biggest challenge that I have in my work is to help people overcome preconceptions and misconceptions about certain products. If retirees are to have a reliable income for life, the proper funding of that income strategy requires that we use various financial products for their best attributes.

THE MYTH OF MARKET PERFORMANCE

In fact, many people hold tight to a myth that the stock market will provide the growth that they need to sustain income throughout retirement. They believe that the sun will always shine on their portfolios. History and statistics tell a different story. Even during good market performance eras, equity investors do not receive all that the market has to offer.

The myth that we could all expect 8 to 10 percent returns seems to be substantiated by the performance of the market. But as I noted earlier, a recent DALBAR study found that the actual return that investors received over the preceding 20 years was far less, which raises the question: Why weren't they getting the full market performance?

Some people hold tight to the myth that the market will give them what they want when they want it, and they think they know what the market has done historically. However, people's personal results show otherwise. The results of the market during your retirement is all that matters, not what has happened historically. The market returns myth fails to account for normal market cycles and the timing of your retirement.

"Some people hold tight to the myth that the market will give them what they want when they want it, and they think they know what the market has done historically."

An extension of that myth involves a belief in a safe withdrawal rate, typically 4 or 4.5 percent of one's portfolio per year. William Bengen in the early 1990s developed the safe withdrawal rate. The rationale was that you could withdraw that much with a high probability of safety. Note, however, that the supposedly safe rate is based on historical US returns. What happens to that rationale when you add in the returns of other developed countries such as Japan, Belgium, France and Germany? If you believe that the world economy is beginning to level the playing field, the historical safe withdrawal rate could be dramatically lower.

All investors must keep in mind the principle of "sequence of return risk"—that is, if the market takes a major hit early in your retirement while you are withdrawing money from an account that fluctuates with the market, you could find it next to impossible to ever get back to even. That happens primarily to people who, in retirement, think it is just fine to use the same investment methods that they used to accumulate their money during their working years.

The people who come to see me generally are the ones who have a desire to take their pile of money and convert it into retirement income. They ask, "Do I have enough? How do we make this work? How do we get an income that will allow us to actually retire and remain retired?"

At this point, we first need to understand their goals and objectives and then get a clear picture of the different methods for creating retirement income. Then, as one of our clients put it, we have to get really granular; we have to get down to the nitty-gritty to really understand the mechanisms that need to be in place for an income plan to work effectively.

HOW MUCH DO YOU NEED EVERY MONTH?

It seems such as simple question: "How much do you need every month to be comfortable in retirement?" It's just a number. What complicates that concept, however, are all the unanswered questions it evokes. What if this? What if that? Still, we need to begin with at least an approximation of that number in mind.

Figure out how much you are spending now, or subtract your savings from your total current income. Then subtract any income source that will disappear once you retire. That will give you a basis for moving forward in your planning.

If we determine that you need $5,000 a month, we'll subtract from that the known income sources you will have in retirement, often in the forms of Social Security, a pension, or rental income if you are confident it will be coming in. The resulting figure is the difference between the income need and the income sources. In other words, it is how much additional income you need.

The most critical factor in retirement planning is time and timing. It is important to understand how to take your pile of money and convert it to multiple uses, connecting the asset with the expense. That is the essence of income planning. That's where we begin to figure out how much of that pile of money needs to be converted to income needs, how much could remain at risk, and how much might be available for passing on to loved ones or charity.

THREE INCOME PLANNING METHODS

The American College of Financial Services, in its retirement income certification program, the RICP course, defines three distinct methods for creating retirement income. In other words, it defines three ways to turn that pile of money into an income. These are the three:

- Systematic withdrawals
- Flooring or baselining
- Bucketing

They all can work, and they are viable income strategies. One or another will work better depending on the needs of the client and the economic environment that we are in. Let's take a look at each method.

"The RICP course, defines three distinct methods for creating retirement income."

Systematic Withdrawals

Systematic withdrawals are what people typically do when they talk about the 4 percent safe rate for pulling income from their account, which we discussed at the beginning of this chapter. There are a number of tests and methodologies within this. It is a very sophisticated strategy and most advisors aren't aware of all the nuances. It is very often misinterpreted and ill-defined, creating the myth that simply taking a predetermined percentage of retirement assets each year will yield a successful outcome. And that's why I have come to believe that it is a myth for many.

Basically, every year, you would determine what percentage of your portfolio you could safely withdraw that year without risking running out of money. The historical withdrawal rate has been under fire and is not an effective rule of thumb. This strategy can work if you take the time every single year to monitor the correct safe withdrawal percentage and adjust your spending accordingly to how the market has performed. You have to do that every year until you die, and so does your advisor.

Most retirees really aren't equipped or interested in that kind of a strategy. It can be very dangerous to use that strategy without a full understanding, especially when markets decline and you are withdrawing income.

If the market is declining, you have to face up to the fact that you need to withdraw considerably less income. That can be confusing because the market often rebounds. But ultimately, the income needs to be less. The safe withdrawal rate percentage can often be more, but the income needs to be less because it is a smaller portfolio than it was the previous year. That alone sounds contradictory, and it adds to the confusion of this really complex income strategy.

What we find is that advisors and clients want to consider that strategy because it sounds elegant and simple. It also generally avoids using annuities and that's a bad word to some people.

Flooring

Also called "baselining" or "essential versus discretionary," this income planning strategy can be as simple or as complex as you wish to be. Basically, it involves converting a portion of your pile of money to a floor of income. It is called "flooring" or "baseline" because you are building that floor or base of income that secures your essential lifestyle expenses. Any additional money can be left at risk to hedge inflation and provide for your discretionary expenses.

The income floor is the income you know is coming in, and typically, you would tie that to what you know are your basic lifestyle expenses. Any extra money that doesn't need to go into building that income floor could be left at risk in the market. You could leave the money at risk, and then you could layer income on top of that floor to address peaks or high levels of spending in any particular year or period.

If conditions are right, a sophisticated series of bonds with staggered maturities can be used for flooring — basically, laddering a bond portfolio to create a floor of income. An alternative strategy is to use a lifetime payout annuity.

The problem with an immediate annuity is that most people do not like the idea that if they die too soon, they have given all that money to the insurance company and the insurance company keeps it at their death.

The bond strategy is one that, again, is very sophisticated and to implement requires somebody who really knows what he/she is doing. In times of rising interest rates, bonds may not be the safest strategy due to the risk of reinvesting maturing bonds in a rising interest environment.

Flooring using an annuity can be a very effective strategy if you do not want to monitor and maintain your plan throughout retirement, and you do not mind the possibility that you might die too soon and thus leave a lot of money with the insurance company.

Bucketing

The third strategy is called "bucketing," which, in a way, is a combination of the first two, with a twist. We use a very specific form of bucketing called the sequential income planning system (SIPS). Bucketing provides a base of income that's guaranteed for the rest of our clients' lives. We use guaranteed products to build that base, but rather than commit to one floor of income or one particular product or an annuity, we use a series of products in successive order in various buckets.

The first bucket, for example, would represent your needs in the first five years of your retirement. That bucket would be funded with a very safe, often guaranteed, type of product that would allow you to spend that money down until, after five years, that bucket is empty.

While you are spending that guaranteed money for the first five years, the second bucket has been left alone to grow uninterrupted, and thus can earn a higher return because you've given it time.

Then, once you've reached that sixth year, you begin spending the money in the second bucket, and all the while you have had a third bucket funded with a guaranteed account—generally, a fixed annuity that provides income for life for both spouses.

What's really noteworthy about this strategy is that you will know exactly how much money you will get every year for how long by building that strategy. If you were to die early, all of the money that hasn't been spent passes on to your beneficiaries, guaranteed, because you haven't turned those buckets into income at that point.

If you are fortunate enough to have additional money, you could leave it in a risk position in the market. Why would you do that? If you opted to leave it at risk, you could choose investments that typically would counteract inflation. The safe and the guaranteed products that are used to build the bucketed income, the sequential income plan, are generally not geared toward high levels of growth. They are designed to create high levels of income. That is their best attribute.

If you pair those with investments that are designed for potential growth, and you give them plenty of time, it is likely that any inflation can be offset by the growth of those investments that are at risk in the market. We have studies showing that the pairing of guaranteed products with risk-based portfolios, when managed correctly, create the greatest probability of success of a retirement income plan. There are a lot of moving pieces, in theory, but once you set it up, the income is certain.

SIPS bucketing is really a combination of systematic withdrawals and flooring or baseline, but it is what has been working most effectively now for many retirees. The method has received a lot of attention because it works, as proved by the data.

A Better Cash Flow

As you can see, you can arrange your finances for far more peace of mind in retirement than you can get from the traditional strategy of systematic withdrawals. The "safe" rate, after all, is before you pay any investment fees or taxes. If you subtract those amounts, and if you think more globally, the safe withdrawal rate is actually much lower than the 4 percent originally theorized in the 1990s. Several studies indicate the safe withdrawal rate is around 1.8 percent.

"As you can see, you can arrange your finances for far more peace of mind in retirement than you can get from the traditional strategy of systematic withdrawals."

A person who has a $500,000 portfolio using a 1.8 percent safe withdrawal rate could safely withdraw $9,000 per year. My prospective clients laugh when I share that number with them and ask them, "Is that okay? Would you be able to live on that?" They are incredulous, but that's what the data is showing. It is not, however, what most advisors are telling people.

The SIPS methodology, by contrast, generally will generate an income plan for clients with a cash flow well above 5 percent. The reason that people do not want to do this when they first learn of the strategy is that it involves guaranteed products such as annuities that have gotten a bad rap, because they are often used for the wrong reasons.

At the end of this chapter, I will give some specific examples of how retirees use SIPS bucketing. First, let's look at some other concepts and income strategies that you should understand as we create your comprehensive retirement plan.

LIQUIDITY, SAFETY AND GROWTH

If we step back from these different planning strategies, there are three overriding themes or aspects to financial planning that need to be reflected in your income plan. Those are liquidity, safety, and growth. It is critical to make sure that each is represented by the investments in your retirement plan.

Liquidity means you have access to your money. You need to have access to your money when you have an expense, so it is unwise to lock all of your money up so that it is unavailable when you need it.

On the flip side, and this may surprise you, you want to avoid having too much liquidity. The result of that will be an inadequate rate of return. If you have access to every dollar in your portfolio every day of the week, there's a very good chance you are giving up long-term growth by choosing to have unlimited liquidity. You need a balance.

Most of our clients really want safety. They want guarantees. They want certainties. The problem with too much safety is you lose the potential for growth, because if you never take a risk, you never grow, or so the theory goes. Safety needs to be adequately accounted for in an income plan, but we also need some growth in the portfolio to counteract the forces of inflation and potential health-care costs.

It is often said that you can choose any two of those three—liquidity, safety or growth—because an individual investment can't provide all three. But let me suggest that you indeed can have all three or the potential for all three if you take a variety of investments that are suitable for specific purposes and invest them sequentially over the period of your retirement, 5 years, 10 years, 15 years into the future. After you spend the money in your initial income bucket, it is replenished by money in the later growth buckets. That way you can take advantage of the growth as well as having the liquidity for your immediate needs and financial security so that you can sleep at night.

By properly using bucketing in the form of the SIPS program, you are getting all three. The personal pension part of it, the income plan that's guaranteed, gives you safety, because you cannot lose your money. You cannot lose a dollar of that part of your savings, because it is in products that are guaranteed—that is, so long as the company backing them maintains its financial strength.

Liquidity comes in the form of pairing the different time segments with your financial assets. You need liquidity in the first five years, because that's the "now" of your retirement. For your second five-year period, you may not need as much liquidity now. So the money you are reserving for that period can, in the meantime, be invested appropriately for greater gain. That money will become available—it will gain its liquidity—just when you need it.

You can still have the element of growth. It is represented in the money that's outside the income plan. We do not want to put every dollar into the income plan if we do not have to. We want to keep some out of the income plan to grow better and keep up with inflation.

The percentages and proportions of liquidity, safety and growth are different for every client, but I think they all should be represented. You need a detailed analysis of your needs, your assets and your risk tolerance so that we can bring it all together into a unified whole.

THE "RECOVERY" BUCKET

Many retirees are in favor of leaving an inheritance for their loved ones and or charity, but first they want to know that there will be enough for themselves. And that's wise. It's the rationale you hear when you're on an airplane: "In the event of an emergency, secure your own air mask before helping the person next to you." If you are not okay, you can't help others.

Retirees could get that assurance right away with the guarantees of the sequential income planning system. In fact, they likely will get an income a few percentage points above what they would have under the systematic withdrawal strategy. They could earmark that extra money to potentially pass on to loved ones, without losing access to it themselves. They could do that because the guaranteed strategy would bring them a greater cash flow and money that they wouldn't have to commit to their income plan.

We call that the "recovery" bucket. A recovery bucket contains the money that you now can set aside for loved ones, if you so desire, because you have "recovered" it from your own income needs.

THE RIGHT PRODUCT FOR THE RIGHT NEED

To customize a financial plan to serve individual needs, we need to overcome biases about whether certain products are inherently good or bad. Like my daughters, they most certainly are different, each with different strengths. Some financial products serve to produce liquidity and income, some offer greater protection of assets, and others are designed for growth or for tax deferral.

"Some financial products serve to produce liquidity and income, some offer greater protection of assets, and others are designed for growth or for tax deferral."

Nonetheless, if you take a quick tour of Google, you can find a slew of articles and videos slamming just about every financial product out there. Somebody has a bias, or an ax to grind, or is trying to create a sensational headline to get your attention.

In fact, I have blogged on that very subject, because it presents such a problem for retirees. They do not know whom to trust.

Sometimes when they see a video or read an article bashing a product, they assume the advisor who offers the product no longer is trustworthy.

Remember always that the person making such recommendations has not reviewed your personal financial situation. It is important to be discerning about what you come across on the Internet. It is not the product but how it is used that determines its effectiveness. The proper use depends on your unique needs, and a good advisor needs to specialize in helping people in your stage of life and must get to know you personally.

Variable annuities, for example, often get a particularly bad rap, but again, no product is a rip-off by definition. Let's say you are a physician who makes hundreds of thousands of dollars per year, and you have an incredibly high tax rate. You've maxed out your 401(k), you have no opportunity to fund IRAs, and you are looking for any kind of tax-deferred growth you can find. A variable annuity may be a good fit because it offers tax-deferral and potential growth for a high-income earner.

A variable annuity has some benefits of value, even if they are not for many people. What happens is that oftentimes a product such as a variable annuity is sold to people who shouldn't be buying it. The people who should be buying it might never even consider it because they have been told that it is bad. It is not a rip-off by design. Would you pay 4 percent fees each year to reduce the tax burden on the growth of your million dollars? There's a mathematical, factual reason to say, "Yes. I would consider that." Most people who are buying them, however, are doing so for the wrong reasons.

Variable annuities, which were once extremely desirable, are not as competitive with other products right now because of the dynamics of the economy. That doesn't make them bad. It just means they may not be the most suitable product for most people right now.

The job of advisors is to evaluate what is working now. Their firm has to be set up so that they can get access to the most competitive products. That's where we come back to the suitability versus fiduciary standards, to the independent versus the captive agent. If the captive only works for one company, it is very possible that the products that company offers are not the most competitive at that moment.

I believe being an independent advisor lets me be agile so I can use the right products at the right time, depending on the economy and individual circumstances. That can make all the difference. As a specialist, I must have professional integrity and do the research needed to stay on top of matters.

"Being an independent advisor lets me be agile
so I can use the right products at the right time,
depending on the economy and individual
circumstances. That can make all the difference."

WHAT ABOUT SOCIAL SECURITY AND PENSIONS?

Social Security still accounts for a big percentage of the income for most retirees. If a couple needs $5,000 a month and will be getting $2,500 in Social Security income, they have an income need from their other assets of $2,500.

A lot of retirees are very concerned about whether Social Security will even be there for them for the long haul. That's a valid concern for people in their 20s or 30s. For somebody who is nearing retirement, I think it is fair to assume that Social Security will be there. Social Security's own website suggests that in the year 2036, the system will only be able to pay out 77 percent of current benefits. That's the year someone who is 43 today would reach full retirement age.

Social Security benefits might be reduced for younger people, but generally, people who are already getting benefits will continue to get them. It's the younger people that the system's financial problems are likely to affect. Most people nearing retirement are not thinking of Social Security as icing on the cake. They are planning for the benefit to be a significant percentage of their income.

Many retirees also are counting on a company pension, but those defined benefit plans are quickly becoming a thing of the past. Most people now have to build their own pension to meet their income needs and stay ahead of inflation.

With such uncertainty, many retirees wonder what age they should choose for retirement. "If Social Security could change," they ask, "and if pensions aren't what they once were, how do I know when I can retire safely and comfortably?"

Sixty-two is well known as the earliest age at which somebody can draw Social Security benefits, and that's considered an early retirement age for Social Security. At this point, for most people, full retirement is at 66 years of age or older.

Let's say you choose to take it at age 62. You are going to get less income and less benefit. Roughly speaking, every year that you wait to get Social Security income after age 62, you will grow your income by 7–8 percent.

If you took Social Security at 62 instead of at your full retirement age, you would most likely be giving up about 33 percent of your benefit. If you waited until age 70, you could add another third on top of it. There's a dramatic difference between claiming at 62 and waiting until 66 or 70. Every person is different in terms of what is the right answer.

The question always comes back, "What is the breakeven? If I wait until 66, at what point will I be happy that I did that? How long do I have to live for that to have been a wise decision?" The answer depends on a number of factors, and we have software that can help retirees decide what is best for them. A lot of people claim early because they say, "Well if I die, I want to at least get my money back," so it is an emotional decision. Others who claim early say, "Well I think Social Security is in trouble and it might not be there." Nonetheless, for a lot of people this is the majority of their income, and the claiming decision needs to be made wisely.

Step back and recognize what retirement income planning is: preparing for the possibility that you might live a really long time. If you are not going to live a really long time, there's really no reason to plan. Spend it all. If you are going to live a really long time, you must plan.

We need to put Social Security decisions in the context of "what if I live a really long time?" What if you live well into your 90s or into your early hundreds, which is becoming more and more probable, statistically. When you put it in that context, deferring Social Security until at least full retirement age or beyond begins to make a lot of sense because of the added income that you'll receive by waiting. Social Security has been consistently offering cost-of-living adjustments. The bigger the benefit that you get by deferring, the bigger the raise you'll get through cost-of-living adjustments.

You can defer until 70. After 70 there is no additional growth. Nonetheless, most people take it at 62. But most really should wait until they are 66.

Again, we are all about customizing strategies to fit individual needs, and to say that everyone should wait till 66 would be wrong. There are sometimes reasons why claiming at 62 makes sense. You may be forced to retire due to downsizing; you or someone in your family may have a health issue. There are very good reasons to claim early, and that's why the provision is there.

For people who have the choice to defer, ask yourself this: "Do I think my other investments will grow more than 8 percent per year?" If they are not guaranteed to grow more than 8 percent per year, you are taking a risk by not deferring Social Security. By claiming earlier, you could take less out of the retirement accounts, sure, but it is likely that your retirement accounts won't grow as quickly as the money that you would have earned by deferring Social Security.

People are inclined to look at the numbers today. To get $200 a month more by waiting a year or two or three might not seem like much, but if you live into your 90s, that can become tens of thousands. It could become a six-figure difference.

Your spouse's age is another consideration. If you were the principal wage earner, you will get a significantly greater Social Security benefit than your spouse. If you are the man and your wife is several years younger than you, remember that women, statistically, live several years longer than men. Because she is younger, and has greater longevity, she could be collecting spousal support benefits for many years after you die. And she will be collecting significantly more if you defer your benefit.

Working an additional year can significantly increase your retirement income in more ways than just the greater deferred Social Security benefit. Every year that you can postpone withdrawing money from your nest egg, the more that money can grow. Let's say you are 62 and earning $80,000 a year. You've saved half a million dollars, and it is earning 5 percent on average. If you wait one more year before retiring, you earn an additional $80,000 of income and you save a year's retirement expenses of, say, $50,000. That's money that won't have to come out of your nest egg now, and it is gaining interest of $2,500. When you add it up, it means you actually are making $132,500 by choosing to work one more year. And then you can also factor in the 7–8 percent boost you get in your Social Security benefit by waiting an additional year. If you are questioning whether you are going to have enough to retire, one more year will make a profound difference in your overall retirement income. Knowing that, you might have a whole new outlook as you head off to work in that last year.

"Working an additional year can significantly increase your retirement income in more ways than just the greater deferred Social Security benefit."

PUSHING THE RETIREMENT BUTTON

It is an exciting day when you can push that retirement button and turn on your income plan to move into the next phase of your life. We want to make sure that you will be making the most of your nest egg and that means carefully allocating your assets by those time sequences that we discussed in the "bucketing" strategy, or SIPS. Let's take a closer look at how that can work.

To keep it simple, investments in the first five years typically will be any type of guaranteed product that the client is comfortable with. That could be a fixed immediate annuity that's designed to have a five-year payout. It could be CDs if that's what the client wants. It could be cash. It could be anything that's guaranteed. Some of our clients will choose to take a little bit of risk in that first bucket. They'll invest in a conservative income portfolio. It is a professionally managed portfolio with a combination of short-duration bonds, dividend-producing stocks, and master limited partnerships. Those are designed to create income without significant risk.

The setup for the second five years could be similar. Some clients will choose to put annuities into both of those buckets. However, in theory, the second bucket can be invested a little more aggressively because you are giving it five years to grow. Today, most of our clients who have witnessed the recent economic turmoil are interested in guaranteed products in those first two buckets. In fact, most of them want guaranteed products in the third bucket, as well, and leave the risk-based money entirely outside the income plan. Every client is different.

The third bucket, which is for use after ten years, is really the most critical. It needs to sustain you for the rest of your life, guaranteed, no matter how long that is. If you are married, it has to last as long as your spouse lives too. That calls for a specially designed product. We typically use a specially designed annuity product in that third bucket. Here's why: An annuity offers something that nothing else can offer: a guaranteed lifetime income. Imagine telling a stockbroker, "I want you to guarantee that my money for the next decade will grow at 6 to 7 percent every year, and once I decide to start taking income from that account, I want it to last for my life and my spouse's life, contractually guaranteed. And if either of us needs a nursing home stay or home care, I want you to double our income for up to five years." The broker would laugh. That's not what he does. But that's what this type of annuity product in that third bucket can do. That's a powerful foundation to put underneath your income plan.

Once we fund those buckets, you can choose to turn to invest-ments that do well in hedging against inflation. You might dedicate a portion of your savings to inheritances and charity. If health care remains a concern, you might allocate even more to that. You can budget for a new car, or the new roof your house might need. Those are a few examples of the higher level budget items you might decide to fund.

In developing these retirement plans, we use the best technol-ogy that we have been able to find. We employ the talents of people nationwide who, with your permission, will help us build the best possible plan. That means if I get hit by a bus, your plan still works because you've got a team of people who know how the plan runs, they know what it is designed to do, and they will make sure it does what it was promised to do.

HOW ONE COUPLE FARED

We determined for one couple that they would need about $80,000 per year to continue their lifestyle into retirement. Each had Social Security benefits, and they had some rental income. Altogether, they had an income of about $44,000 heading into retirement. They needed $36,000 more, even before we factored in inflation. They had accumulated just shy of $1.5 million. That was the pile of money that we had to work with to come up with that difference.

Had we done the systematic withdrawal strategy, the safe withdrawal rate of 4 percent, they would have needed to use $900,000 of that money to generate that $36,000 in income. By building their SIPS plan with all guaranteed products, we were able to fund it with only $588,546, which generated a 6.12 percent cash flow to produce $36,000 per year. That's significant, because it meant they had to devote a much smaller portion of their nest egg to attain their desired income. The difference was $311,454.

In addition, the income was guaranteed for both of their lives, and if either of them needed long-term care at some point, the plan would create an additional $36,000 per year on top of that income for up to five years. Meanwhile, that $311,000 difference they did not need to allocate to income could be added to their remaining money and could be allocated to risk-based investments if they wanted. It could create a nice bequest to their children, grandchildren, church, or charity. It could pay for an Alaskan cruise, a second home—it would help with whatever they wanted to do in retirement.

Not only did they have to allocate less of their nest egg to producing an income, but that income was certain. This is all possible when retirees become clear and deliberate about goals and strategies for retirement. We like to call the certain and guaranteed income your mailbox money. On the same day every month, you put on your robe and your slippers and walk to the mailbox, and there's your check. The next month, and the next month, your mailbox money arrives, steadily and reliably.

FINDING THE BALANCE

Income planning can sound daunting. It can feel downright frightening. The ability to create something that is certain, that is guaranteed, can bring incredible peace of mind to a couple who are facing a once-in-a-lifetime decision. The details can be as complex and complicated as you would like them to be, but the process and methodologies can be very simple.

I would warn you, however, to work with somebody who specializes in working with retirees. We want to make sure we choose the right types of products, in the right proportion, and for the right reasons. Be sure that the advisor is equipped to walk alongside you. You need to have a team in place that will support the planning so that it is done factually and logically and not just with a heavy dose of hope.

Just as in music, timing is everything. Rhythm is that underlying force that brings out the color, the shape, the beauty. The income plan is much like that foundation of rhythm in music. Applied correctly, it allows you to move forward freely and fully. You feel assured of a successful performance. You're not just hoping it turns out okay.

My grandma lived with my family when I was younger. She lived with us the last two years of her life, and she passed away just before her eighty-sixth birthday. She and my grandpa were of the depression-era mindset and had scrimped and saved and done without a lot of things in order to have something for the future.

In those last years, my grandma spent next to nothing. She would occasionally try to put a $20 bill into my mom's purse to pay for pizza for the family on a Friday night, and she always wanted to keep the candy dish full, but really her expenses were very low. With all that scrimping and saving, she left a fair amount of money behind.

It seemed kind of sad, quite frankly. We are all trying to get to that point where we know we are going to have enough and won't run out of money, but we certainly do not want to do without all of the things we dreamed of for our retirement. It's a balancing act, and it takes finesse. But when you find the rhythm, you find what is meaningful. You can live more fully, and you can help others to do the same.

CHAPTER 7

Finale: Determining Your Legacy

"If you don't design your own life plan, chances are you'll fall into someone else's plan. And guess what they have planned for you? Not much."

—Jim Rohn

---

lfred Nobel, the Swedish chemist who invented dynamite, was stunned one morning by the obituary he read in the newspaper. It was his own. The newspaper had confused him with his brother, Ludwig, who had died.

Even worse than seeing his own name in the death record was reading how the newspaper described him: He was a "merchant of death." A merchant of death? Nobel had thought dynamite would end all wars by making them too dreadful to contemplate.

From that day forward, Nobel resolved to create a different legacy by which he would be remembered. He wrote a will leaving everything to establish the Nobel prizes for human accomplishments. He had been given a rare opportunity to glimpse how others would see him after he died.

How will you be remembered? What will be your eulogy? Good financial planning means that you will die with money left over. Would it not be wise, then, to begin with the end in mind, as Stephen Covey famously said in his Seven Habits of Highly Effective People, and do some planning for those dollars that outlast you? It is there that we have an opportunity to plan our legacy and how we will be remembered, beyond the dollars and cents.

WHY ESTATE PLANNING?

All of this underscores the importance of estate planning and being mindful and deliberate about your estate, and how it will be managed if you become incapacitated or die. A surprising number of people believe that they don't have an "estate" because they don't have millions of dollars, and that only the very wealthy have one that calls for planning. That is really not the case. Your estate is all of the property you own, including real estate, bank and investment accounts, retirement accounts, vehicles and even life insurance. Most people end up realizing after meeting with us that they are wealthier than they thought, when everything is added up. When you factor in pensions and the present value of Social Security, and how that plays into your estate, you may be even more surprised.

In planning your estate, you generally are intending to pass on assets as effectively and efficiently as possible to the people or to the organizations that you care most about. You hope to exercise some authority in that distribution, not just for the sake of controlling the assets but often to protect those who will receive it.

In the event that you were to pass away tomorrow, would the person receiving those assets be ready for them? There may be some planning to be done to protect them from themselves and from the burden of money that they do not yet have the skills or maturity to manage. There are countless stories of second- and third-generation family businesses that fail miserably because the recipients of the wealth just weren't prepared. They couldn't handle the weight of those financial matters.

FOR FAMILY AND CHARITY

When I talk to people who are retiring today, they frequently are concerned about what will become of the future generations. Most people reading this book will have some pension or Social Security, and some accumulation in the form of IRAs or 401(k)s. For people in the generations ahead, those income sources are in jeopardy. We touched on Social Security problems lying ahead, and most pensions just do not exist for workers entering the workforce today. They are forced to save on their own.

Through effective estate planning, those future generations can better receive the benefits that you put in place for them. Many people do want to help the next generation if they can, and they are open to planning for that. They begin thinking of who matters most and where they can create a benefit, make an impact, and leave a legacy. Then, after deciding just whom or what they want to help, whether family members or charities, they get into the nuts and bolts of how to do that most efficiently.

TIME TO REACH OUT

Medical advances have allowed people to live significantly longer than past generations, and many retirees, through good fortune and prudent saving, have an unprecedented opportunity to live well for 20 or 40 years without working. If that describes you, congratulations.

With that asset of time, however, comes the responsibility of using it wisely. Estate planning, when done correctly and early, can help you to feel confident that you actually will have assets to pass on. That's when you can start devoting the necessary time and take the steps to be sure that the next generation will understand what it took for you to create that wealth. You want your heirs to know what that wealth means and the best way to make use of it.

The Rockefellers and the Carnegies and others of the Industrial Revolution did a phenomenal job at building into ensuing generations an understanding of the responsibility for wealth. They were the builders of great libraries and other institutions. They devoted significant effort to grooming the next generations to be able to manage and to steward the wealth they created. They wanted their heirs to understand what it meant to have wealth.

Once you identify who is most important to you, you can deepen your relationship to help them understand what to do with that wealth they will receive. Estate planning is very much legacy planning, and it involves a lot more than money. It involves values, attitudes, beliefs, and what matters most to you. Money should be a means to an end, a tool to do greater good. A good steward is concerned about relationships and takes the time to be sure that his/her treasure advances truth as he/she knows it. Today's retirees, who often will have years at their disposal, will do well if they take the time to reach out.

"Estate planning is very much legacy planning, and it involves a lot more than money. It involves values, attitudes, beliefs, and what matters most to you."

GETTING STARTED WITH ESTATE PLANNING

How does one begin this process? First, be clear that you want to do it. It can be as deep as you want to go. You start by getting documents in order: all those investment statements, pension and Social Security documents, insurance policies, wills, trusts, powers of attorney. By pulling everything together, you can begin to look through the lens of how you want your assets to be handled during your life and after you pass.

"This sounds like it is going to be exhausting," some clients say. And it can be, quite frankly. It can be exhausting, but it is followed by a sigh of relief. Often for the first time in years, they will have a basic understanding of all the assets in play and how they can work together to create the desired outcomes. When they leave with a binder full of strategies and plans, they then can visit with an estate planning attorney.

They are on their way to the peace of mind and security that comes from knowing the planning they put in place will allow their legacy to continue. People can live more freely knowing their affairs are in order. In fact, doing so is a selfless act. You are making sure that those you care about will not be burdened with any conflict over your final intentions.

As for the nuts and bolts of developing an estate plan, I highly recommend that you work with an attorney who concentrates on it. Like every other facet of financial planning, or any business for that matter, there is so much to understand. Because things change so quickly, you need to work with someone who stays current with the latest issues and has the experience to help you identify the pitfalls and opportunities.

Let me be clear: I am not an attorney, and I do not offer legal advice. In my practice I recommend that my clients seek the counsel of an experienced estate planning attorney.

THE BUILDING BLOCKS

The first decision, then, concerns whom you would like to leave your assets to. After that, you need to consider the best ways to distribute those assets and get them to the recipients. With the counsel of an estate planning attorney, you can answer those questions together.

I have encountered a number of cases in which none of the basics of estate planning had been addressed. Not only were the documents not in order but they did not exist. Perhaps there was an intention to draft a will, but it wasn't done. Or, more commonly, a will was created when the kids were young, and it hadn't been updated in decades. I sometimes joke with new clients about that. "So do you have a will?" I ask. "Or, let me guess. It was last updated in 1984 when the kids were young, right?" Typically, they checked documents off their list long ago, did a will, got health-care power of attorney and other papers, and figured they were set.

But a lot changes in life, and a lot changes in the need to plan. Think about the dynamics of a modern family. With so many divorces and remarriages, a lot of people have not planned for the second, third, fifth child. Some people are excluded from an estate plan who should be included, and vice versa.

"A lot changes in life, and a lot changes in the need to plan. Think about the dynamics of a modern family."

It is always a good time to update an estate plan, and it makes sense to do it in conjunction with your retirement planning since you already have those documents in one place. You can integrate the planning and give it the attention it deserves. We prefer to work with estate planning firms that offer a maintenance program so that you have an incentive to consult with them once a year to update the plan. That helps to assure that any changes in your dynamics or your wishes are factored into your planning.

What are the building blocks of an estate plan? There are many facets, but the most basic documents include wills and trusts.

To explain the basic tools used in estate planning, and how to evaluate the choice of one over another, I've enlisted the help of my good friend and trusted estate planning attorney Richard Chamberlain. Richard is relentlessly focused on educating people on the need for and the tools involved in properly planning an estate. He strives to protect assets as well as safeguard the wishes of those who have worked so hard to provide for others financially. For over a decade, Richard and I have been aligned in serving clients in a comprehensive fashion. Here are his comments on this issue. (For more, visit www.chamberlain-law.net.)

RICHARD CHAMBERLAIN ON "A WILL VERSUS A TRUST"

Q: What's the Difference between a Will and a Trust?

That's one of the questions I hear most often from people when they first sit down with me. As an attorney concentrating in estate planning law for the past 15 years, I know that this information is critical as people begin their estate planning. I'm grateful to Adam for asking me to address this question in his book.

At their most basic levels, Wills and Trusts perform a lot of the same functions. They both contain instructions for how a person's assets are to be distributed when they die, and they both nominate the people who will be in charge of handling the estate. For this reason, I often refer to a trust as a "will substitute."

There are two fundamental—and crucial—differences between wills and trusts. I'll list them briefly, and then explain each one more fully in turn.

1. A will only operates in probate court, but a trust can be used to avoid probate.

2. With a trust, you are able to build in protections for your beneficiaries, but with a will you cannot.

Avoiding Probate

For some people, one of the most important aspects of using a trust is avoiding probate. Some of these people have been through the probate process with the estate of a loved one and know firsthand why probate should be avoided. Others have only heard that they should avoid probate, but don't know why.

There are three primary reasons why people want to avoid probate (in my office we call them the pitfalls of probate):

- **Expense**—Probate can be a very expensive process. The legal fees charged are based upon the value of the assets in the probate estate, and in our area they can start as high as 4 percent of the first $100,000 of probate assets.

- **Lack of Privacy**—Probate is a public court process, so any person can look at the information in a deceased person's probate court file. This includes (1) the names and addresses of the heirs and beneficiaries of the decedent, (2) specific information on all assets in the estate owned by the decedent, and (3) detailed information on how the estate was distributed.

- **Lack of Control**—The probate process is designed to have a person's estate be administered and then closed as soon as possible. Assets are distributed from the probate estate to the beneficiaries from the probate estate, and from that point the beneficiaries are "on their own" to make good decisions about how to invest, save and spend the assets. In many circumstances, people need to be able to do more to protect their beneficiaries (as shown in the next section).

When people have more information on probate, they generally look for ways to design their estate plan to keep their estates out of that system. A living trust can be used to avoid probate and the pitfalls associated with the probate process.

Protecting Your Beneficiaries

One of the most powerful aspects of using a trust for estate planning is in protecting your loved ones.

In some situations, our clients will design their trust to make an outright distribution to their beneficiaries. This plan is appropriate if the clients feel that the beneficiaries are mature enough and secure enough to receive the inheritance outright. In other situations, however, an outright distribution may not be the best way.

The question I ask my clients, as it relates to beneficiary distributions, is whether they need to protect their beneficiaries from certain "life risks" that exist now, or that may exist in the future. By designing the trust in a way that does not give an immediate outright distribution to the beneficiaries, the clients are able to provide the necessary protections for their beneficiaries.

There are several different categories of life risks that your beneficiaries may face, or may be currently facing. Some of these categories include:

Creditors—whether they have creditor problems now, or some that arise in the future.

Predators—people who would take advantage of them after they receive an inheritance.

Poor financial judgment—sometimes our loved ones just aren't good at handling money.

Loss of benefits—if you have a loved one with special needs, the wrong kind of estate plan could cause them to lose the benefits they depend on.

Divorce loss—if one of your loved ones got divorced, would you want their ex-spouse to receive half of their inheritance? Without proper planning, that can happen.

By using a trust for your estate plan instead of a will, you are able to create a plan that is customized for the needs of each individual beneficiary. Your trust plan can have provisions protecting your loved ones from these and other risks that can affect them.

Q: Should I Have a Trust?

Again, this is a question I hear a lot. Ultimately, the answer to that question depends on your needs and goals. But generally speaking, a person should seriously consider a trust-based estate plan if they can answer yes to one or more of the following questions:

- Do you want to simplify your estate for your loved ones and make it easier for them to administer everything after you've passed?

- Do you want your estate to stay out of probate?

- Do you have any concerns about any of your beneficiaries (if they would receive a lump sum inheritance from you)?

Though having a trust plan can help you simplify the administration of your estate, there are a lot of issues to consider when deciding if a trust is right for you, and how it can be used to meet your planning needs. In order to make that determination, you should consult with an experienced estate planning attorney to discuss these issues and apply them to your individual circumstances.

—Richard Chamberlain

COST VERSUS BENEFITS

So why would you not do estate planning? Generally, people have a reservation about paying for it. However, estate planning can be a powerful vehicle and the cost can be low relative to the benefits created, especially if you have even a modest estate. Every attorney will charge a different fee for estate planning, but generally you are looking somewhere between $1,800 and $3,000 for a living trust-based estate plan. That includes the basic documents, including the trusts and the health-care powers. You can build a really solid plan for that amount of money. When you compare that to what could be lost, it really makes a lot of sense to sit down with an estate planning attorney and investigate your options.

Once people learn about probate—how expensive it is, and how public—they become more interested in estate planning and the use of trusts. You can avoid probate by funding your trusts so that you no longer own the assets. That means by establishing trusts while you are alive, you can save the money that would have been required to have the estate administered through probate. You may well want to spend the pennies to avoid paying the pounds.

"Once people learn about probate—how expensive it is, and how public—they become more interested in estate planning and the use of trusts."

TAX ISSUE IS CHANGING

Taxation is another significant variable that must be addressed in estate planning. Most people believe that when doing estate planning, the estate tax is the one to focus on. That's the tax levied by the federal and state governments on the value of your estate exceeding a certain amount.

Not long ago, the federal estate tax credit or exemption went up significantly. A couple who do just basic planning can have over $10 million of assets without being charged any federal estate tax when they pass away—some call it the death tax. Fewer and fewer families right now are facing an estate tax at the federal level, and my state, Ohio, recently repealed its state estate tax.

However, what people are missing is the fact that most of the wealth that people have in their estate is in tax-deferred accounts, such as 401(k)s, or 401(k)s that became IRAs, or tax-deferred annuities. All of the income taxes on those assets that were deferred for decades will become payable by the beneficiaries in most cases. Uncle Sam will want his cut and often will be taking it when the money goes to the heirs. If they receive it as a lump sum, they may get significantly less than expected.

Therefore the real issue is not the estate tax any longer. Much of the challenge now is to plan for the income tax that is due when an estate passes from one generation to the next. The tax issue has changed, and unfortunately, a lot of advisors aren't even talking about it. We think it is a major concern, and we are regularly working with accountants and estate planning attorneys in recognition of this ticking time bomb of tax-deferred accounts. With proper manage-ment while you are alive, you can maximize your own benefit and how much goes to charity and minimize the tax burden on your beneficiaries.

"The tax issue has changed, and unfortunately,
a lot of advisors aren't even talking about it."

CHARITABLE STRATEGIES

Are you charitably inclined? Are you interested in helping a cause or charity? That desire is different for everyone, but there are planning strategies that could allow you to give more money to charities without disinheriting your family. The byproduct of that strategy is that to a large degree you can actually disinherit Uncle Sam legally. You can carve him out as the major beneficiary of your wealth and replace him with a charity of your choice without taking anything away from your family members. There are planning strategies that can allow that to happen.

Instead of the government distributing your wealth for what it decides is the public good, you decide for yourself how your assets will be distributed for either the public good or the good of your family. You maintain control. Most people are less than pleased with all the ways that the government chooses to distribute tax money for public benefit. By being deliberate in your planning in regard to charities, you can minimize your taxes and target how a lot more of your money will be utilized.

As I progress in a planning relationship with a client, I often will ask, "Do you have any charitable inclinations?" Everybody is different, and I do not pass judgment. But in either case, I point out that there are strategies to benefit charities that would actually create a greater net wealth for the giver. There are still significant tax benefits from giving money to charities.

One reason that retirees might resist giving to a charity is they don't know enough about it to be certain the money would be used well. That, of course, can be investigated, but it's really more than that. First, clients want reassurance that they will be okay themselves. That's when they will be open to the possibility of helping others. And that's when they can see that proper planning provides powerful tools for tax advantages.

Nonetheless, once they reach that point, I often find that people are trying to give away the wrong money. An estate will usually have a variety of types of assets. There are assets that have been tax deferred. There are assets that have already been taxed. Often, people are getting their income out of their retirement plan. They are paying taxes on that. Then they are giving to their charity of choice out of their income. But in so doing, they meanwhile are allowing tax-deferred assets to continue to defer. When they pass away, they give their heirs the tax burden they put off.

"I often find that people are trying to give away the wrong money."

Instead, if you want to give money away, you could donate some of those tax-deferred assets to the charity. Remember that charities are tax exempt. Where you or your loved ones would have to pay tax on those assets, the charity does not. You can plan to give your tax-free assets to your children and grandchildren.

"If you want to give money away, you could donate some of those tax-deferred assets to the charity. Remember that charities are tax exempt."

Let's say you have life insurance in your estate. Life insurance passes on to your beneficiaries tax-free because of the nature of life insurance. If you want to help a charity out of income, what you can do is give away some of the tax-deferred assets on which you or your heirs will have to pay taxes. By giving the money away, you get a tax deduction for your gift to charity. You can use the money you gain from that deduction to pay for a life insurance policy. The payout on that life insurance will go tax free to your heirs. It's not hard to see why that is a far more efficient strategy than simply giving away assets on which you already have been taxed.

In other words, why give money that is not going to be taxed anyway to an entity that doesn't have to pay taxes? A little bit of wisdom, a little bit of foresight, and a bundle of money can be saved there.

There are a lot of charitable planning strategies, but it begins with caring enough for a cause to make it all happen. That's why the first question is whether you want to pursue charitable giving. If so, then we can investigate strategies. If not, no problem, but you still may want to look at strategies available to maximize assets left to your children and grandchildren.

IN SEARCH OF SUCCESS

This comes back to those same themes that I bring up early in conversations with all my clients: What are their goals? What do they want to do with their lives? What is important to them? You have to know that before you can do any sensible estate planning.

What is your definition of success? It can be a difficult question to answer. We get our idea of success through media images, from family, by our upbringing. And yet no matter how often we are told what it is, we often haven't decided for ourselves.

It's a step you can't skip. The definition of success in your planning has everything to do with the outcomes. By defining goals, you can become much clearer about the right tools, strategies, and options available for achieving them. You will know whether to take along the chainsaw or the Swiss Army knife for your journey.

Success is less about money and more about those that we care about and relationships with our family members and our community. The money becomes a vehicle to more clearly and more powerfully express our beliefs and help others. Money is indeed a powerful force. It is powerful in that it gives us options. We can choose to use it for great good and that underscores the importance of understanding the true meaning of success.

Will any plan be perfect? No. That is why we periodically update your plan. Our goal is to help you to be more deliberate. New influences and new experiences shape all of us. We must get to the core of what we want to accomplish. With such power at our disposal, we must be clear about the relationships we wish to positively influence. We must know whom we hope to help.

"New influences and new experiences shape all of us. We must get to the core of what we want to accomplish."

I love the detail, the strategy, the process. People hire us to do that for them. They trust in our competence and our specialization. Most clients want to be sure we know what we are doing, but they don't want to know how to do it themselves or else they would. What they truly want is to live more fully, confident that the plans are in place.

"WELL DONE ..."

In the Bible is the parable of the three servants each of whom was given a portion of his wealthy master's fortune for safekeeping when the master went away on a journey. One of the servants buried his portion, while the others invested and increased theirs. The master, upon returning, scorned the one who buried it. He had not lost it, but he had not made the most of it.

To whom much is given, much is required. Each of us, I believe, is required to make the most of God's portion for us and put it to the best use. When we have more, more is expected of us. We have hands and feet for a reason. It is indeed a lot of work, but those who are good stewards will rise to the challenge. The matriarchs and patriarchs of their families will feel a sense of responsibility and pride.

It is not supposed to be easy. We all need to be reminded of that, myself included. Life can be challenging, but it is supposed to be meaningful. It is supposed to matter. We should reach out to serve, and we should do right with what has been entrusted to us. One day we will be called to account. For me, I can only hope that my reward, upon my passing, will be to hear the words, "Well done, good and faithful servant."

CONCLUSION

The Unified Whole

"I never worry about action, but only inaction."

—Winston Churchill

What is music, anyway? It actually doesn't make sense, and yet it is universally understood. In Western music we have all agreed that a certain progression of notes is the foundation of all musical performance. We have agreed about rhythm, structure, notation.

I had a wonderful opportunity to perform with the US Air Force Band in Hungary. We played a joint concert with a Hungarian military band. They could not speak our language, and we could not speak theirs. We sat next to our counterparts, who were playing the same kind of instruments that we were, but we couldn't even say,

"How do you do?" But what we could do was play. Hungarian and American, we looked at that sheet music, and we could perform the same piece. Despite our cultural gap, we spoke the same language in music. We agreed on the building blocks, the fundamentals.

Music is powerful yet mysterious, something that makes no sense, yet makes all the sense in the world. What would our world be without the music? I cannot conceive of that. Yet one could argue that music serves no practical purpose.

Retirement is a relatively new concept. Generations past worked until they died. Today's retirees can anticipate living for decades beyond their working years, with money as their store of value and means of exchange. Like music, the value of money is ethereal. Its true value lies in how we use it, and what it means in our lives. And like music, money has rules and fundamentals that we must observe to get the most power out of it for generations to come.

"Like music, money has rules and fundamentals that we must observe to get the most power out of it for generations to come."

In this book, I have outlined some of those rules and strategies for planning an income that will last a lifetime and beyond, but most critical is this question that each of us must ask: "Who and what is important to me?" What will you do with all that you worked so hard to attain, with all that has been entrusted to you, with all the blessings of a lifetime?

When we can answer those questions, we are moving beyond the question of what money means. We are asking instead what it means to love one another, to serve one another. In one sense, is money not simply a certificate of our service to others?

We can fully live when we see wealth as a means to effect positive change in our families, our relationships, and our communities. And when we are gone, our loved ones will look at our years on earth and say, "What an amazing life."

"We can fully live when we see wealth as a means to effect positive change in our families, our relationships, and our communities."

That's the fruit of compassion and purpose. That's when we have found our unified whole.

A TIME TO ACT

I remember it vividly: We were sitting in the doctor's office in Columbus when my wife was having a difficult time in her pregnancy with the twins. We went to see a specialist. The twins were struggling. We were given a course of action. We could allow one of the babies to be terminated in order to save the other. We had to make a decision.

We had to take action. In the end, we recognized that these were not our children coming into the world. It was not for us to decide if one should go.

WE ARE SIMPLY CARETAKERS

We decided that our action would be to put them in God's hands. We would do everything we could to get them as close to the finish line as we could, but life, or death, would be God's will.

When we are faced with what to do next, it is rarely a matter of life and death. Still, the choices that I am encouraging you to consider in your retirement planning and your estate planning are no small matter. They have significant weight to them. You have in your hands the power to help or to hurt, not only yourself but others too.

This is a time to act. This is a time to get down to some serious decisions with the counsel of those who know what you are facing. I urge you to act, confidently and diligently, so that you can attain the peace of knowing you did your very best with all that was in your care.

Appendix

and supporting items (organized by chapter)

CHAPTER 1

Shell Oil Retirement Longevity Study

"Mortality improved with increasing age at retirement for people from both high and low socioeconomic groups," they found. "Retiring at 65 was not associated with a greater risk of mortality than retiring at 55 or 60."

The findings appear in the online edition of the *British Medical Journal.*

TEDX—Dan Buettner: How to Live to Be 100+

Centenarian study cited: "In the Okinawa language, there's not even a word for retirement. Instead, there's one word that imbues your entire life and that word translates roughly as 'the reason for which we wake up in the morning.' The centenarians in the study were able to answer this question instantly."

The Allianz Reclaiming the Future Study

"A surprising 61% of all respondents said they were more scared of outliving their assets than they were of dying. That number climbed to 77% for those aged 44-49, and rose even higher (82%) for those in their late 40s who had dependents."

CHAPTER 2

Risk Analysis Example

In order to determine the actual amount of market risk present in a client's existing portfolio, an analysis can be run to measure the standard deviation and average return for a given investment portfolio. The result allows the clients to see how much their portfolio could lose in a 2008-like market crash or how much their portfolio could gain in a late 1990s bull market. The analysis is measured in dollars and percentage and also highlights the standard deviation in the portfolio, a statistical measurement of the risk present in a portfolio. This allows the client to avoid guessing and making assumptions about the risk present and decide if adjustments to the portfolio are desired.

The $758,782 investment portfolio in this example could lose approximately 35 percent or $265,000 in the worst possible market conditions or it could grow 53 percent or $401,000 in the best possible market conditions.

Another way of looking at this is to ask whether, in an era of very low interest rates for very conservative investments (US treasuries), you would be comfortable owning a portfolio during retirement that is attempting to earn 9 percent each year. Each client is different and each scenario deserves a high level of scrutiny. Since past performance is no guarantee of future results, this is simply one measuring device that retirees should be using to develop their retirement plan.

Current Risk Analysis

Historical Standard Deviation Chart for the Current Investment Holdings

Portfolio Value:	$758,782
Average Return:	$9.00%
Standard Deviation:	14.65%
Current Risk:	Moderately Aggressive

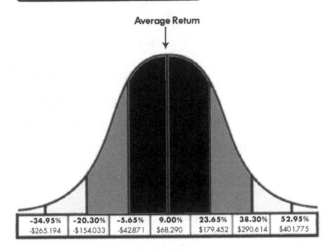

Average Return

-34.95%	-20.30%	-5.65%	9.00%	23.65%	38.30%	52.95%
-$265.194	-$154.033	-$42.871	$68.290	$179.452	$290.614	$401.775

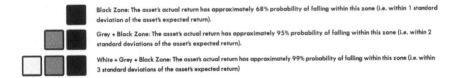

Black Zone: The asset's actual return has approximately 68% probability of falling within this zone (i.e. within 1 standard deviation of the asset's expected return).

Grey + Black Zone: The asset's actual return has approximately 95% probability of falling within this zone (i.e. within 2 standard deviations of the asset's expected return).

White + Grey + Black Zone: The asset's actual return has approximately 99% probability of falling within this zone (i.e. within 3 standard deviations of the asset's expected return)

Current Risk Analysis supplied by permission of Global Financial Private Capital, an SEC Registered Investment Advisor

CHAPTER 4

Fiduciary versus Suitability

Broker (the suitability standard)

- Represents the company, not the client;

- Offers products for sale from a range of products carried by the company he/she represents;

- Is paid commissions calculated as a percentage of the amount of money invested into the product;

- Only needs to check the suitability of a prospective buyer, based primarily upon financial objectives, current income level and age, in order to complete a commissionable sale of a financial product.

Advisor (the fiduciary standard)

- Represents the client, not the company;

- Offers "best advice," taking into account the needs of each individual client;

- Is paid a quarterly fee calculated as a percentage of the assets under advisement;

- Requires advice to be provided in the best interests of the client including the disclosure of possible conflicts of interest.

Sure-Fire Steps to Hiring the Right Advisor

Do They Specialize?

Determine if a specialist is your best choice. Does he/she work with anyone or is he/she focused on working with people who can address your specific needs? Does he/she maintain credentials and certifications in that specialization?

Don't Go It Alone

Does your advisor encourage collaboration with other professional advisors? An advisor who is open to working with other professionals has additional checks and balances that could ensure your plans remain on track.

Understand Your Advisor's Fee Structure

Do you fully understand how the advisor is being paid? Learning the difference between a broker (suitability standard) and an advisor (fiduciary standard) will help you ensure your interests are aligned.

Demand Proof

How do you know your advisor's advice is trustworthy? Before acting on financial advice, assess the advisor's competence by asking some key questions. How that person answers the following "Five Critical Questions" should give you a good idea of his/her qualifications and passion for his/her work:

Five Critical Questions to Ask Before Acting on Financial Advice

1. Have you adequately reviewed my personal financial situation to confirm this recommendation is in my best interest?

2. How will your plan affect my tax return each year and what future tax issue may concern me?

3. How will your plan affect my income and liquidity needs in the future?

4. How does your plan match up with my risk comfort level?

5. How will your plan affect the transition of my assets to my heirs?

Trust Your Instincts

When in doubt, step back and reconsider. It is very seldom that quick decisions with your life savings will be rewarded. It is also critical that both spouses are confident with the choice of advisor. In retirement planning, it is very likely that the widow will be interacting with the advisor at a very difficult time. Therefore, a trusting relationship is essential.

CHAPTER 5

27 Major Retirement Risks
(RICP® curriculum, The American College)

1. Longevity risk

2. Excess-withdrawal risk (also called portfolio failure risk)

3. Inflation risk (also called purchasing power risk)

4. Timing risk (also called point-in-time risk)

5. Long-term-care risk

6. Frailty risk

7. Heath-care-expense risk

8. Investment risk

9. Asset-allocation risk

10. Market risk

11. Sequence-of-returns risk

12. Reinvestment risk

13. Liquidity risk

14. Legacy risk

15. Forced-retirement risk

16. Reemployment risk

17. Public-policy-change risk

18. Loss-of-spouse risk

19. Unexpected-financial-responsibility risk

20. Financial-elder-abuse risk

21. Unrealistic-expectation risk

22. High-debt-service risk.

23. Procrastination risk

24. Overinvestment-in-employer-stock risk

25. Rollover risk

26. Retirement-saving-opportunity risk

27. Inadequate-resource risk

The Effects of Rising Health-Care Costs on
Middle-Class Economic Security

> Harriet Komisar, AARP
> January 2013

Family Health Costs Rise 5%

> Jeanne Sahadi, CNNMoney.com
> September 15, 2009

The Real Cost of Owning a Mutual Fund

> Ty A. Bernicke
> April 2011

The Hidden Costs of Mutual Funds: Portfolio managers can
rack up steep expenses buying and selling securities, but that
burden isn't reflected in a fund's standard expense ratio.

> Anna Prior, *Wall Street Journal*
> March 2010

Genworth Financial: Compare Cost of Care Across United States

> Genworth.com

An International Perspective on Safe Withdrawal
Rates: The Demise of the 4 Percent Rule?

> Wade D. Pfau, PhD, *Journal of Financial Planning*
> May 2011

Say Goodbye to the 4% Rule

> Kelly Greene, *Wall Street Journal*
> March 1, 2013

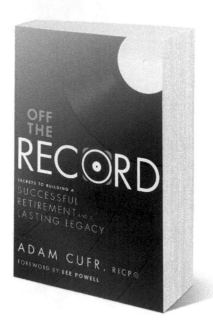

How can you use this book?

MOTIVATE

EDUCATE

THANK

INSPIRE

PROMOTE

CONNECT

Why have a custom version of *Off the Record?*

- Build personal bonds with customers, prospects, employees, donors, and key constituencies
- Develop a long-lasting reminder of your event, milestone, or celebration
- Provide a keepsake that inspires change in behavior and change in lives
- Deliver the ultimate "thank you" gift that remains on coffee tables and bookshelves
- Generate the "wow" factor

Books are thoughtful gifts that provide a genuine sentiment that other promotional items cannot express. They promote employee discussions and interaction, reinforce an event's meaning or location, and they make a lasting impression. Use your book to say "Thank You" and show people that you care.

Off the Record is available in bulk quantities and in customized versions at special discounts for corporate, institutional, and educational purposes. To learn more please contact our Special Sales team at:

1.866.775.1696 • sales@advantageww.com • www.AdvantageSpecialSales.com